321 S STATE
WIN—E

# A Brief
# History of
# Psychology

# A Brief History of Psychology

**Michael Wertheimer**

*University of Colorado*

**HOLT, RINEHART AND WINSTON, INC.**

*New York    Chicago    San Francisco    Atlanta*
*Dallas    Montreal    Toronto    London    Sydney*

# Preface

The late Karl F. Muenzinger (1885–1958) felt that study of the history of psychology could help the student develop an integrated overview of the field, which might serve to reduce the perplexing, apparently unrelated, diversity of the material encountered in various psychology courses. Accordingly, he prepared a course in the history of psychology, which was for many years required of senior majors in psychology at the University of Colorado. While his course to some extent followed Edwin G. Boring's (1886–1968) *A History of Experimental Psychology*, which Muenzinger typically used as a text for his course, he developed some innovations that students found useful—such as an identification of eight major trends which culminated in the birth of experimental psychology. I was privileged to share with Muenzinger in the teaching of the course during the mid-1950s. This experience helped further to consolidate my interest in the history of psychology, originally sparked by Robert B. MacLeod and by Edwin G. Boring, and also sustained by my contacts with O. J. Harvey.

In my last conversation with Muenzinger, not long before his death, he asked that his outline be used in any way that might be appropriate. The present manuscript reflects Muenzinger's course in part, with many changes, some minor and some not so minor. Most of the basic structure is Muenzinger's, but much of the superstructure and details are from elsewhere. And Boring, shortly before *his* death in 1968, wrote a detailed commentary on the manuscript, making many useful recommendations, most of which have been incorporated in the book. Julian Jaynes, of Princeton University, also read the manuscript and made useful suggestions.

The material has been tried out at several institutions, in lecture form and in mimeographed form with undergraduate and graduate classes in the history of psychology since the fall of 1962, and student reactions and suggestions, for which I am grateful, have been used in revisions of the manuscript. Some parts of it have been presented at colloquia at various colleges and universities, as well as at American Psychological Association conventions.

Because the presentation is brief and condensed, it has usually been accompanied in my courses by assignment of a standard text such as Gardner Murphy's *Historical Introduction to Modern Psychology* or Edwin G. Boring's *A History of Experimental Psychology*.

In conjunction with a book or two of readings in the history of psychology, like some of those mentioned in the reference section, the book may perhaps serve as a text to hold a course together. Alone, it might be useful to anyone wishing a quick overview of the history of psychology, perhaps an interested layman or a graduate student who wants his memory traces tickled in preparing for examinations.

Boulder, Colorado                                    MICHAEL WERTHEIMER
November 1969

# Contents

# A Brief
# History of
# Psychology

# 1

# Introduction

Before we set out on our brief tour through the history of psychology, let us pause for a moment to consider some general background. The first section of this chapter will raise a few questions about the nature of history itself, and about the problems that one will inevitably encounter when he takes on the role of historian. The next section presents some thoughts about why one should bother with contemplation of psychology's history in the first place. Finally, the third section explores the various ways in which the history of psychology has been organized, referring briefly to some of the better known works in the field, and ends with a characterization of the approach taken in the present work.

## SOME COMMENTS ON HISTORY IN GENERAL

The historian faces obstacles the scientist can avoid. Historical truth is more elusive than scientific truth, although the scientist has his problems too. Paradoxically, a historical "fact" changes, but an empirical statement of a relationship stays put in some sense: anybody can check it. Scientific knowledge is timeless; a scientific generalization can be tested any time, by anyone who cares to set up appropriate conditions for observation. But history is an all-or-nothing affair; something happened once, and that is that—you cannot bring past events back into the present to study them and their determinants and effects at leisure, turning them this way and that, as you can examine some scientific statement in the laboratory. To be sure, there may be relics of the past event that you can use to try to pin it down—letters, canceled checks, diaries, monuments, official documents, sales slips, or the Congressional Record—but none of these is the event itself, and none is of unquestionable reliability or validity. Most important, none really tells you how to interpret the event. You can't unequivocally determine the causes and effects of the event, can't manipulate the independent variables responsible for it nor measure the dependent variables it affects. In fact, you never can be sure that the presumed event actually happened at all. Perhaps it's just the figment of someone's desires, dutifully perpetuated by those who came later. Chances are, it's harder to break a fad in history than in science.

Quite aside from questions like whether Columbus discovered America in 1492 (or whether it was Amerigo Vespucci, or a foolhardy Norseman, or, for that matter, the indigenous Americans, who were unaware that their land had to be discovered), there is the question of the *importance* of a presumed event. It is primarily this aspect of history which changes. How important was William the Conqueror in determining the events of 900 years ago? Just how significant is the Boston Tea Party *really?* Should everybody know how many soldiers went with Cyrus on the third march of the fifth month of his Anabasis, or how many accompanied Caesar from one part of Gaul to another? It may be intriguing to hear that Hannibal managed to prod a herd of elephants over the Alps, that Henry VIII had goodness knows how many wives, and that Demosthenes stuttered; but, ultimately, so what? Rather than recording that a man once stood at a graveyard and intoned, "Four score and seven years ago," and so forth, why not record that an ant, at the same time and place, happened to be walking over the letter *M* on poor Private Joe Smith's headstone? That's an event too. History just isn't impartial; it is highly and inevitably selective.

History, then, deals with events about which one can't be sure, whose significance is anybody's guess, and whose selection for attention is an idiosyncratic, subjective matter. No historian can be unbiased. Even if one had many lifetimes, and infinite powers of observation and memory, it would still be an impossible chore to produce a complete, unbiased description of all of the events that occurred, say, between 11:01 A.M. and 11:03 A.M. on Friday, September 6, 1968. What do you include? That President Johnson sneezed? That Rachel Wallach, sitting in her living room in Durham, North Carolina, scratched her left knee? That a new satellite was launched from Cape Kennedy? That in Rocky Mountain National Park a 13-inch diameter piece of granite, loosened by the freezing and thawing of thousands of years, fell with a clatter (barely missing Jonathan Hough, the distinguished mountain climber) from near the top of the East Face of Long's Peak down onto Mills Glacier, and then rolled all the way into Chasm Lake? And even if all of these items were to be included in your list of events, how much detail would you devote to each? How much would you emphasize each one? How far back before 11:01 and how far beyond 11:03 would you go in order to "make the event meaningful," to "set it in its context," to "show its significance?"

No, history is not independent of the historian. It does not stay put. Which event to emphasize, which one to include or exclude, how to interpret what you select—all of this depends upon the historian's bias.

Much of what the student of history has to wade through is the doings that somebody thought important, of people whom somebody thought important. Perhaps the easiest, and clearly the most usual solution is to write about people considered significant by their contemporaries, and events that at the time caused raised eyebrows, an increased heart rate, or untimely deaths. Kings, dictators, presidents, prime ministers, religious leaders and their wars, battles, murders, intrigues, and other shenanigans form the bulk of most history books. Some daring souls have also tried histories of ideas, of cultural movements, of man as a thinking, creative, evolving creature, rather than a purely political or economic one—a rather different orientation. Yet the basic problem remains the same: how do you select, what do you relate to what, how do you interpret what? Somebody else may see the same things very differently, or may choose to look at very different things.

One recurrent issue, insistently and insightfully brought by Edwin G. Boring [1950 (b)] to the attention of anyone interested in history, is that of the Zeitgeist vs. the Great Man view of events. Just what is the role of the spirit of the time (the Zeitgeist) or of the place (the Ortgeist) in determining what happens, as against the role of some unusual person, who is strong enough to withstand the Zeitgeist or the Ortgeist and change the course of events? Was Freud just a passive agent of the climate of ideas in Vienna at about the turn of the twentieth century? Would somebody else have come up with an emphasis on unconscious motivation, or was he, his unique existence, responsible—in spite of the Zeitgeist—for the creation of the psychoanalytic view of man? It is usually too simple to cast such questions into an either-or form; but the relative contribution of the great man and of the Zeitgeist still remains largely a matter of the intentional or unintentional raw preference of the historian. Even though there may be occasional circumstantial evidence, such as simultaneous independent yet similar discoveries or formulations, which suggest a Zeitgeist influence, there are no real, objective guidelines to help him.

And then there is the question of the organization of what the historian chooses to pull out of the stream of events. Chronology seems the obvious outline. But it is not really as straightforward as all that. If the historian tries to make some sense out of what he is talking about, rather than record in an endless, dull list that this happened, then that happened, and then the other occurred, he must permit himself to jump back and forth to some extent. While he is busy expounding the chain he has constructed for events q, r, s, and t, he must ignore the fact that u, v, w, and x happened to be going on at the same time—according to his view, they belong in a different chain. So he runs back again to u, v, w, and x after he has finished with q, r, s, and t. The extreme of a pure chronology, then, is just about impossible, even if he breaks his account down into arbitrary units such as the period 1740–1749, then 1750–1759, and so on.

The other extreme is completely separate chains, as in one book about the history of England and another about the history of France, or one on philosophy and one on psychology. But this approach also has inherent problems. Most historians will want to refer to other concurrent chains occasionally, especially when they happen to have links in common—as in the invasions of France by England or vice versa. Again, it seems a matter of sheer preference whether the historian chooses to be closer to the chronology pole or the history-of-some-particular-movement (or country, or discipline, and so forth) pole.

These points are raised here partly by way of defense. The present writer is not a professionally trained historian. But if history is at bottom a matter of idiosyncratic bias concerning what to include, how to include it, and how to interpret it, then even an amateur's effort may be permissible. To the extent that it differs from others' efforts, it might help to loosen a possibly too-tenacious tradition of what the best way to systematize the field might be, or of what "the" history of the field is. There is no such thing as "the" history of anything.

## SOME COMMENTS ON THE HISTORY OF PSYCHOLOGY

Yet the history of psychology is enjoying a popularity it never had before. As of the present writing, there are now more books about it in print than ever before, and more have been published in the last few decades than in all the preceding time. Almost every introductory psychology text touches on it. There is a *Journal of the History of the Behavioral Sciences* and an Archives of the History of American Psychology, and the American Psychological Association has a Division on the History of Psychology, all of them established during the 1960s.

This upsurge of interest must have a reason. Psychologists are expected to know something about the history of their discipline, and a course in the history of psychology is part of the requirement structure for the undergraduate psychology major at many colleges and universities. Particularly when one considers that all too many people view history as a dull subject, a matter of memorizing undifferentiated concatenations of names and dates, why encourage—or force—exposure to such dry and deadly material, possibly running the risk of snuffing the student's intrinsic interest in the subject matter of psychology because he may generalize a negative valence attached to endless detailed chronology? Why is it widely held to be a "good thing" for the student of psychology to have some acquaintance with the history of the discipline?

First, there is Cicero's rationalization, engraved in stone over the door of the University of Colorado's Norlin Library, that "who knows only his own generation remains always a child." Mankind and human thought have evolved over the eons, and the incredible spurt of progress in the last few centuries has doubtless been greatly helped, perhaps even made possible, by the practice of preserving one man's ideas in writing so that another man, or many other men, could ponder it even when the original author of the idea was not around. To grow up, one needs to extend his horizons beyond his own limited sensory experience.

And yet one could counter that there may be harm in smelling the grey mustiness of bygone times. Perhaps this is the route to becoming a bubble, an empty Babbitt, to losing childhood's saturated enthusiasm, to acquiring an unproductive, level-headed, resigned, perspective-filled maturity and the conviction that there is nothing new or worthwhile under the sun.

Another reason sometimes given for studying the history of psychology is that it is traditional to do so. Even Aristotle's *De Anima* has a section on preceding philosophers' musings about the soul. Titchener inspired many about the importance of psychology's history, and just about all teachers of psychology had to take a course, at one time or another, in the history of psychology. So, the argument seems to go, let us twist the golden rule a bit, and insist that we should do unto others as others have done unto us. Maybe some depth psychologists would point to the security-providing benefits of ritual, but just because something has been done in a particular way for a long time that doesn't mean it is still reasonable to continue doing it. The teaching of today should fit the needs of today; maybe a sabertooth curriculum should be permitted to become extinct with the sabertooth tiger.

Third, the study of history can provide perspective and humility. Knowing that there are points of view different from that to which I am committed, and that others in the past have entertained notions similar to my own, may help me develop my ideas without too much autism. Also, the chances are that ideas placed in a context will be more forceful, fecund, and consequential than ideas developed in a vacuum. Other than pointing to the possible motivating power of blind fanaticism, it is hard to argue against the desirability of perspective and humility.

Fourth, every now and then a study of history can be illuminating about some past mistakes. Hopefully awareness of some of the traps our forefathers have fallen into will make us tread more cautiously, and make it less likely that we will be caught by the same ones.

Fifth, a rather compelling rationale for the study of the history of psychology has to do with the vastness and complexity of the field of psychology today. The typical student of psychology, graduate or undergraduate, finds himself bewildered by the variety of materials he encounters in lectures, seminars, books and journals, all of them presumably somehow relevant to that apparently senselessly conglomerate area known as "psychology." How are the various ideas, subfields, and specialties related? How do they tie in with other disciplines? A historical examination of the field may help integrate, may show how psychology developed out of a rather limited number of fundamental philosophical and scientific concerns, and may help him to see that the seemingly infinite diversity of the disparate things that go under the name of psychology may not be quite as much of an accidental hodgepodge of unrelated facts and theories as it first appears.

Today's psychology is the child of yesterday's psychology; today's psychology makes more sense if one understands how it got to be the way it is. History determines to some extent the problems that are studied and how they are studied, and even the language to be used in talking about the problems. History can help one realize that these things are all the consequences of essentially arbitrary decisions made by people long ago, rather than necessarily inherent in the subject matter itself.

Study of the history of psychology, then, can provide perspective, can point out lines of development, can indicate the origin of ideas, can help one avoid mistakes somebody else before him made, and can show how various things fit together. But ultimately, history, like art, needs no defense. The best reason for bothering with it may well be sheer curiosity, or a desire for the finite bit of flesh to find some meaning in its labors, indeed, in its existence, to transcend its here and now, to discover its place in the vast scheme of things. Just what pleasure and consolation the historian and his consumer get out of the enterprise may be lost in some Freudian impulse, Adlerian complex, or Jungian archetype. Is it a feeling of power, of identification, of being less the victim of one's past if the past is not so shadowy and awesome, like an amorphous apparition, all-powerful in a nightmare? Perhaps knowledge of the past, having a structure for what has gone before, will free one from nameless childish fears and make one able to stride forth on his own, in his own direction. Some psychoanalysts say that an understanding of one's early experience will help one to discover himself, and will make for free, productive endeavor. Maybe an understanding of the early experience of one's discipline—especially if that discipline is concerned with the study of man and his mental life—will have a similar effect.

One need not, though, rummage around in a speculative unconscious to defend the study of the history of psychology. Everybody enjoys a good story. And the history of psychology has some fascinating men and ideas in it, enough for dozens of gripping movies, TV shows, or historical novels. Quite aside from that, it can be very interesting in itself. The study of history, in the last analysis, needs no defense.

## APPROACHES TO THE HISTORY OF PSYCHOLOGY[1]

So there are good reasons for looking at the history of psychology. But how should one organize it, how present it? Several different strategies have been used. Most popular is perhaps the chronological account, exemplified by Boring [1950 (a)] and Murphy (1949). To be sure, these are really quasi-chronologies, following one trend for a while and then backtracking to take up a different trend, yet time is the prime basis for the organization of these books (although Murphy did append a set of chapters on recent research developments).

Second is an approach that emphasizes the great schools of psychology, which flourished during the first half of the twentieth century. Heidbreder (1933) and Woodworth and Sheehan (1964) represent this strategy, and it is also noticeable, although less prominently so, in the books by Wolman (1960) and by Marx and Hillix (1963). In a sense, it is also the organizing principle behind several surveys of theories in particular subareas of psychology, like Hilgard and Bower's *Theories of Learning* (1966) or Hall and Lindzey's *Theories of Personality* (1957).

A third approach has been to ask prominent older psychologists to write personal or professional autobiographies; this was the basis for the volumes entitled *History of Psychology in Autobiography,* originally edited by Carl Murchison, and recently by Boring and Lindzey (1967). A similar organization, although less concerned with the personal and centered more on the professional contributions of distinguished psychologists, is found in the volumes of Koch's (1959–1964) *Psychology: A Study of a Science.*

Related to this strategy is the "great man" organization, which summarizes the contributions of major figures in the history of psychology. George A. Miller wrote a delightful introductory textbook in psychology (1962) which made extensive use of this approach, and it is the focus of works by Watson (1968) and by Sargent and Stafford (1965).

Then there are the implicit histories, the books of readings in the history of psychology, anthologies which compile excerpts from great writers of long ago and not so long ago. Dennis published a compendium in 1948, and more recently Shipley (1961), and Herrnstein and Boring (1965) brought out

---

[1] Many books are referred to in this section. Most of them provide a quite different, and in many cases a more complete, account of the details of the history of psychology than the present text. See the list of References at the end of this book.

longer ones. Each of the more than one hundred selections in Herrnstein and Boring's work, incidentally, is preceded by a brief introduction that places it in its historical context.

Finally, still another departure begins with decisions about which research fields are significant on the contemporary scene, and then proceeds to an examination of the histories of these. Chaplin and Krawiec (1968) did this for each of several major subfields of psychology, such as sensation, perception, learning, quantitative psychology and personality, whereas Postman (1962) chose somewhat narrower issues, such as cortical localiza- tion of function, repression, hypnosis, the nature and measurement of intelligence, or nativism and empiricism in perception, and asked experts in these problems to write histories of them.

The present manuscript combines the first two approaches with the fourth, and concentrates more on experimental psychology than on other fields. The organization is primarily chronological, but with emphasis on the great men in psychology's history, and with fairly detailed examination of the schools of psychology. Part I looks at the intellectual background that culminated in the establishment of experimental psychology as an indepen- dent discipline, glancing briefly at Greek and Renaissance thought and then developing in greater detail the eight major trends that can be seen as the backbone of the new discipline. Part II centers upon Wilhelm Wundt, as the major exemplar of the new psychology, and explores the intellectual climate of his day; it ends with a glance at American psychology both before and after the world center of psychology moved from east to west across the Atlantic Ocean. Part III presents the major twentieth-century schools of psychology, and ends with an attempt at an overview of the psychological scene as the twentieth century enters upon its final third.

## SUMMARY

There is no such thing as a definitive, correct, unchanging history of anything. What is fished out of the stream of events as worth paying attention to, and how what is selected is to be interpreted, depend ultimately on the idiosyncratic, subjective biases of the historian. Nevertheless, a historical overview of a discipline can provide background, integration, and perspective, and can be absorbing in its own right.

Interest in the history of psychology appeared to be increasing during the second half of the twentieth century. Most histories have been written with a chronological orientation, but there have also been books based on signifi- cant schools, important men, influential works, or major research areas. The present work combines attention to the contributions of important men and concern with major schools in a condensed chronological account.

# PART I

# Preexperimental Psychology

# 2

# Early
# Developments

The history of psychology could, as we said in Chapter 1, be divided in any of a large number of ways. Here it is separated into three major divisions, using the approximate dates of 1860 and of 1900 as the dividers. It was in the year 1860 that Gustav Theodor Fechner published his *Elements of Psychophysics*,[1] which for the first time demonstrated how to make precise measurements of mental events and quantities, and how psychical quantities are related to physical ones. Hence 1860 could be seen as the year of birth of experimental psychology (other historians have considered 1879 as psychology's birthyear, because that is when Wilhelm Wundt first undertook research to discover new facts in what was probably the first laboratory for experimental psychology, at the University of Leipzig; still another candidate is 1875, since Wundt was given space for demonstrational experimentation at Leipzig in that year and so was William James at Harvard). As for the other dividing date, it was at about the turn of the century that psychology emigrated from Europe to make the United States its major residence, so 1900 seems another appropriate cutting point.

Eight great scientific and philosophical trends led to the new experimental psychology of the latter half of the nineteenth century, and continued to characterize experimental psychology in the twentieth. The present chapter, after a brief glance at psychological thought in antiquity, will survey these trends, the five scientific ones (physiology, biology, atomism, quantification,

[1] In a brief work like the present one, it seems inappropriate to engage in the pedantry of citing detailed bibliographic references. Elaborations of most of the material presented in this book can be found in the longer works referred to in Chapter 1.

11

and the founding of laboratories) and the three philosophical ones (critical empiricism, associationism, and scientific materialism). Then the last two chapters in this Part will examine the scientific and philosophical trends in somewhat greater detail.

## THE GREEKS, THE MIDDLE AGES, AND THE RENAISSANCE

The eight lines of development from science and philosophy did not really become clearly discernible until the sixteenth or seventeenth century or even later. Yet hints of them can be found in Greek and Middle-Age philosopher-psychologists; the controversies and cogitations of the ancients contained several of them in embryonic form. In this section we shall touch on some of the great pre-Renaissance men and ideas, to provide a background and to set the stage for the subsequent consideration of post-Renaissance developments.

### Elementism and Antielementism

Among the important early concerns was the question of elementism as opposed to antielementism. One of the best-known early atomists was Democritus, who lived about 400 B.C.; he argued that everything is composed of indivisible, unitary material atoms in constant motion. People, for example, are constituted of soul atoms and of body atoms, the latter qualitatively the same as the former, but in slower motion. In his elementism, then, Democritus exemplified some tendencies toward reductionism (by reducing all existence to a common denominator, the atoms) and toward a mind-body distinction. Another aspect of his philosophy emphasized the role of external stimuli in determining the individual's behavior, raising the question of determinism vs. free will: if our behavior is controlled by outside forces impinging upon us, are we really in control of our own actions?

Among the antireductionists, who held views opposed to those of Democritus, were Thales, Heraclitus, and Anaxagoras. Thales, who lived in the sixth century B.C., was one of the most militant antielementists; he considered water the basic substance, the common fabric of most things in the universe. In contrast, Heraclitus (ca. 540–475 B.C.) held that everything is constituted of fire. There is nothing permanent or fixed; fire is the agent of change. This conception has a peculiarly modern quality, especially if we were to translate fire as "energy." He also argued that things tend to go into their opposites—an idea similar to one held much later by Hegel. Heraclitus emphasized process rather than status, dynamics rather than statics. He taught that the stream you waded in yesterday is different when you step into it today; William James, in modern times, made a parallel statement, to the effect that the stream of consciousness is never the same again; you can never experience the same thing twice. Anaxagoras (ca. 500–428 B.C.) considered neither water nor fire the basic substance; he felt that the irreducible, the smallest unit of anything, is a *relationship*. There is no such thing as permanence or fixity; everything is undergoing constant relational change. In this idea he anticipated Aristotle; his notions, and many of those of Heraclitus and Aristotle, can also be seen as similar to some of the emphases of the gestalt psychologists of the twentieth century.

The Greeks engaged intensively in epistemological inquiry. Originally, the issue was, how do we know? Later, it became how can we know—that is, how can we know we are right? It was particularly the Sophists of the fifth to the second century B.C., down through Socrates, who concerned themselves with this question. Among their arguments was the rather disconcerting one that we can never be sure that we *really* know anything. After all, what are the criteria for the validity of any statement, of right and wrong, of true and false, of good and bad? There are none, independently of certain arbitrary points of reference, assumptions, or premises. And we can never be sure whether our arbitrary points of reference, assumptions, premises, or ends are actually valid.

### Plato

A number of these concerns culminated in the philosophy of Socrates and of his disciple and interpreter, Plato (ca. 427-347 B.C.). Popular in primitive philosophy was a kind of animism, in the form that we become aware of the souls, the essences of things, but Socrates taught that our knowledge of the environment is necessarily imperfect, since it comes via the imperfect avenue of our sense organs, which are subject to illusions. We learn about external objects because they emit faint copies of themselves ("eidola"), which enter our receptor organs. Although the Sophists generally doubted the certainty of the existence of objects in the external world, Socrates and Plato believed in a realm of *ideas,* which are permanent and perfect. The experienced world, they held, is but an imperfect copy of this ideal world, about which we can learn only through matter and the material senses—which contribute all kinds of error. The ideal exists outside of man, independently of him, and is immutable and perfect; our perceptions are, then, only imperfect material copies of "genuine reality."

It is therefore foolhardy to consider sensory experience as a reliable source of knowledge. Far more trustworthy, according to Plato, are rational reflection, meditation, introspection; by these means, one can discern truth and can get to know one's self. Indeed, the self is the only object which one can learn about with any degree of assurance, but the process of gaining self-knowledge is also a difficult one, and one that is never complete. There is, incidentally, an interesting parallel between Socrates' recommendation, "know thyself," and the efforts of some of today's psychotherapeutic methods, including those based upon psychoanalysis and perhaps especially those based upon phenomenological personality theories, such as the client-centered counseling of Carl Rogers or the existential approach of Rollo May.

Consistent with his distrust of the senses and of things material, Plato's analysis of social phenomena (which contrasted rather sharply with the prevalent social theories of his contemporaries) was based upon a classification of men into three categories. He who should have the lowest status in an ideal society, according to Plato, is the man concerned with bodily functions and the satisfaction of organic needs: the servant or slave. Next comes the man of emotion, of "heart," of courage: the soldier. The highest position, that of ruler, is reserved for the contemplator, the thinker, the man of intellect and ideas.

Plato taught that men benefited profoundly from one another; that, as John Donne put it two millennia later, no man is an island unto himself. Man is a social creature, much influenced by those around him. Here one can also discern the seeds of an environmentalism, already touched on by Democritus, which was to grow in the philosophy of the seventeenth, eighteenth, and nineteenth centuries, and to reach its zenith in the formulations of the twentieth-century behaviorists John B. Watson and B.F. Skinner.

Another of Plato's contributions was his clear statement of the mind-body distinction, already in the Zeitgeist and suggested, among others, by Democritus; the problem of the difference between mind and body, and of the relation between the two, has continued to engage Western philosophers and psychologists down to the present day.

### Aristotle

Aristotle (384–323 B.C.) was a pupil of Plato's and a rival of his. He was, as far as we know, the first man to write systematic psychological treatises. His works included, among others, *Peri Psyches,* or *About the Soul* (perhaps more accurately *About the Mind* or, literally, *About the Psyche*), sometimes known by its Latin title, *De Anima;* of senses and sensing; on memory; on sleep and sleeplessness; on geriatrics—the length and brevity of life; on youth and old age; on life and death; and on respiration.

*About the Soul* had a remarkably modern outline: it began with a consideration of the history of psychology and prior systematic formulations concerning the mind and behavior, summarizing the thought of preceding Greek philosophers like Thales, Plato, Anaxagoras, Alcmaeon, and Empedocles. Next came a section on the nature of the soul, or what we might today call personality, followed by a section on the abilities of the soul, in which he discussed the senses of seeing, hearing, smelling, tasting, and feeling. His presentation also considered a "common sense," superordinate to the five, which serves to synthesize the information from the other senses, and to include such things as awareness of form, number, and duration, which are not specific to any of the other five senses. Next there were discussions of thinking and imagination, intelligence, knowledge, needs and motives, willing, and feeling and emotion. His analysis of memory culminated in three primary laws of association, which were to have a significant place in the history of thought ever since: contiguity, similarity, and contrast. That is, one idea calls forth another if (a) when previously experienced they were contiguous in space or time, or if (b) they are similar, or if (c) they contrast with each other.

Aristotle was a general theoretician about nature, and taught that behavior is subject to the same kinds of naturalistic principles as all other natural phenomena. A thoroughgoing relativist, he considered the world as made up of various levels of matter and form, which are defined in relation to each other. There is no fixed form or matter, but matter is the constituents, the elements, making up the form, while form is the inclusive totality whose subparts are matter. Thus, marble is matter relative to the form of the pillar, while in relation to the marble, the pillar is the form. At the same time, however, the pillar is matter to the building, the building is matter to the city, and so on. The higher level is thus always the form, the lower level the matter. (A somewhat similar formulation was to be developed early in the twentieth century by people like Christian von Ehrenfels and Alexius Meinong of the Graz school in Austria and by other antecedents of gestalt psychology.) Aristotle thus argued that every object is both form and matter: form to the lower, matter to the higher. He considered the highest form to be God; He is form to all things, matter to none, and thus provides meaning, structure, and organization to the matter of all the world.

Aristotle, by considering all things to be infinitely reducible via successive, ever finer analysis of form and matter, continued the reductionistic trend (although his version was not as elementistic as some earlier ones, or as some in the eighteenth, nineteenth, and twentieth centuries). Aristotle's formulation can also be seen as an early statement of the molecularist position in the twentieth-century molar-molecular controversy, that is, the controversy concerning the size of the unit of analysis or the conceptual level at which explanation is to be sought.

Another of Aristotle's contributions was the doctrine that all knowledge comes from experience. At birth the mind is a blank wax tablet (a "tabula rasa"); experience writes upon this tablet. Much later, John Locke was to elaborate on this idea. This position has recently been called "empirism."

### The Greek Decline and the Middle Ages

Aristotle was a teacher of Alexander the Great, after whose reign the Greek civilization began to deteriorate. In reaction to this time of crisis, of ambiguity, and of anxiety, two opposite philosophical movements sprang up, Epicureanism and Stoicism. The Epicureans were in a sense the beatniks, the hippies, of their time, whereas the Stoics were more like classical reactionaries; the former seemed at least in part to espouse living in the moment, and to have an iconoclastic devil-may-care attitude, whereas the latter, more soberly ascetic, wished to preserve the order of things as they were and subscribed to a somewhat puritanical acceptance of their fate.

As the Greek culture began to disintegrate, the major religions arose and flourished. People were dissatisfied with the status of their today; several of the great religions, notable among them Christianity, tended to concentrate on the future, and held out the hope that tomorrow will bring a better, more pleasant life, perhaps after bodily death. In the first five hundred years after the birth of Christ, Aristotle was forgotten, and religious teachings held the center of the intellectual stage.

It was not until about 700 A.D. that Aristotle was rediscovered by the Arabs, and it took several centuries for his thought to influence the writings writings of the Church Fathers. The Zeitgeist, as it had been for several hundred years already, continued from then until the Renaissance to be strongly antiempirical and proauthority as a source of truth, with the authority vested almost exclusively in the Church. The rediscovery of Aristotle put thinkers into a somewhat difficult spot, because many of Aristotle's beliefs were inconsistent with religious teachings. For example, Aristotle considered man part of the natural world, whereas religion taught that man was separate and above the animals. It is largely because he managed to come close to accomplishing the difficult feat of reconciling Aristotle's ideas with religious dogma that Saint Thomas Aquinas (1225–1274) stands out as an important figure in the history of ideas.

### The Renaissance

The Renaissance, from about 1400 to about 1600, saw a gradual, subtle, but radical change in man's attitude toward knowledge and toward sources of knowledge. The authoritarianism of the interpreters of Aristotle and of the religious writers slowly gave way to empiricism and antiauthoritarianism. Old, established ways of doing things and of thinking about things began to be questioned. It was also a period of major geographical exploration, of change in the economic system toward a trading economy, and of breakdown of the feudal manorial system, under which man had had his particular position carved out for him by destiny, and did not question the order of things. He had previously accepted as foreordained the particular social, economic, and political niche to which fate had relegated him. Political units became larger and more powerful, and competition—in the economic, intellectual, political, and military realms—became acceptable as individualism arose. Knowledge and a man's status were no longer fixed, but became fluid. Gradually there arose an awareness that one need not accept things fatalistically, but that it might be possible to progress toward a better life and a better understanding of the world.

The Renaissance was an era of ferment in virtually every area of human endeavor. From about 1500 on, a general spirit of expansion pervaded many different spheres. New geographical horizons were opened by Spain and Portugal, and England was in a period of major expansion of its empire. The expansion was not only geographical, but also cultural: it was late in the sixteenth century that Shakespeare began writing. The new dynamic culture flourished in France too, particularly in the French empire under Louis XIV; this was the period of the great French writers Molière, La Fontaine, Racine, and Corneille. Russia pushed its borders all the way to the shores of the Baltic, Charles XII of Sweden explored widely and built his empire, and Prussia expanded toward the East.

The expansionist tendency was not only territorial and physical, spiritual and literary, but also scientific—as shown by the figures of Galileo and Newton. There was also a widening of philosophical horizons, and certain psychological concepts came into being. It is no accident that psychology, like so many other fields, had its major rebirth during the Renaissance, after several thousand years of darkness. To be sure, psychology during this time was primarily philosophical, but many of the trends that were to join to produce the experimental psychology of the late nineteenth century could already be identified in this period.

## SURVEY OF SCIENTIFIC AND PHILOSOPHICAL TRENDS THAT CULMINATED IN EXPERIMENTAL PSYCHOLOGY

During and shortly after the Renaissance there developed as distinct entities the eight movements that were to have a profound effect upon the shaping of the science of psychology. The new experimental psychology arose from the confluence of two great rivers—one a river of science, and the other of philosophy. The tributaries of the river of science were physiology, biology, an atomistic approach, an interest in quantification, and a tendency to establish university research and training laboratories; the tributaries of the river of philosophy were critical empiricism, associationism, and scientific materialism.

### The Scientific Trends

Within *physiology*, there was much work on sense organs, and there were studies that later would have been called neurophysiological. Fascination with man's body led to a detailed study of structures and their functions, and the functional units making up the body were studied in the reflexes of both animals and men. Reaction time was a topic of great interest among astronomers, then physiologists, and later yet, psychologists. The controversy concerning the localization of functions in various brain structures, which is still raging today, was already joined in the first half of the nineteenth century.

The most important *biological* concept, in terms of its influence upon the development of psychology, was evolution. It was there in the writings of Buffon and Lamarck, and it was just one year before 1860 that Charles Darwin published his *Origin of Species*. This influence continued with Spencer, and Darwin himself contributed a volume on the expression of emotions in man and animal.

The *atomistic* approach was surprisingly successful in several different disciplines, so it was only natural that the young psychology too would try to adopt it. Chemistry served as the shining example, with John Dalton's ingenious atomic theory and his classification of the elements.[2] In neurophysiology, there was Santiago Ramón y Cajal's neuron theory, and many philosophers both before and after the days of Aristotle had viewed mental events atomistically, including also an interest in how associations are formed among mental elements or atoms. Associationism, a kind of mental atomism, has been a major movement in the history of both philosophy and psychology.

*Quantitative* thinking in psychology received a substantial nudge in the first half of the nineteenth century. It was then that the discipline of statistics arose, and it is doubtless the quantitative emphasis of the Zeitgeist—especially in physics, the science that the young psychology tried so hard to emulate—that made the acceptance of psychophysics and of mental testing spread so rapidly. Analytical geometry and the calculus were invented long before, and Galileo had quite naturally stated his law of falling bodies in mathematical form.

Finally, the first half of the nineteenth century saw the formal establishment of a series of university research and training *laboratories,* each involving the cooperative work of at least several people. Although there

---

[2] Dalton also made an important contribution to psychology in his observations on color blindness: he happened to be color blind, and provided the first description of the phenomenon, which was called Daltonism for a while. His description arose out of his embarrassment at having bought bright red clothes and worn them to Quaker Meeting, since he was unable to distinguish their color from black.

were laboratories in other fields as well, the movement was particularly characteristic of chemistry. Thus, in central Germany, by 1824 Justus von Liebig, who studied the chemistry of fertilizers and agronomy, formally opened a chemistry laboratory at the university in Giessen; in 1836 Friedrich Wöhler, at his newly established Göttingen laboratory, synthesized the first organic product, urea. This synthesis, incidentally, had the far-reaching implication, which fit into the mechanistic spirit of the time, that organic products can be produced outside the human or animal body: there is no need for a "vital force" or some other mystical entelechy. In 1840 Robert Wilhelm von Bunsen (of burner fame) established a laboratory at Marburg, and in 1843 another chemistry and physics laboratory was founded at Leipzig. The 1840s saw the establishment of a chemistry laboratory at London, as the movement crossed the Channel, and also one at Yale University, as it crossed the Atlantic.

These five scientific trends converged to make the new experimental psychology physiological, evolutionary, and atomistic, with an emphasis upon quantification, and gave support to the establishment of a large number of laboratories of experimental psychology in the last decades of the nineteenth century. But, to repeat, philosophy also had its marked effect upon the new psychology, with three main developments contributing to this impact.

### The Philosophical Trends

The *critical empiricism* movement, begun by the Greeks, was concerned with the logical critique of all experience. Among the important later writers in this tradition are Locke, Berkeley, Hume, and Kant. All were deeply concerned with the question of how knowledge is acquired. A related question was whether there are any innate ideas, or whether all ideas come from experience—the issue of nativism vs. empirism.[3]

The *associationist* tradition concentrated upon the question of what makes ideas hang together; how do ideas bring forth others; how do ideas congeal. There was much concern with how one idea makes one think of

[3]We encountered the word *empirism* at the conclusion of the section on Aristotle. Distinguishing between *empiricism* and *empirism* helps to clarify one's thinking. Empiricism is a methodological prescription: it says we should rely on observation, on experience, on measurement, to obtain reliable knowledge, and contrasts with rationalism, which holds that reason is the best route to knowledge (cf. Plato). Empirism is a philosophical assumption: it says that all human knowledge comes from experience, that no knowledge is innate, and contrasts with nativism. Clearly the two are not totally unrelated, since experience is central to both, and yet they are clearly not identical. One can, for example, be an empirical nonempirist (by doing, say, experiments on inborn propensities) or a nonempirical empirist (by maintaining deductively, or by assumption, that all human behavior is learned, as, for instance, in Aristotle's doctrine of the tabula rasa).

another, how things are learned, how long a once-formed association will last, and what conditions during learning will affect a connection's durability.

*Scientific materialism* consists of the attempt to describe living organisms and their processes strictly as machines, in terms of physical and chemical events. French materialism, as exemplified by Julien de La Mettrie[4] in his work *L'Homme machine,* presented a convincing and disquieting account of man as a machine, both physically and mentally. By the middle of the nineteenth century a mechanistic approach to the understanding of living organisms, including man, was very much in the Zeitgeist. Wöhler's demonstration that one can synthesize organic material out of inorganic, mentioned just above, was typical of this trend.

That the new experimental psychology, then, was much concerned with epistemological questions, was strongly associationistic, and tried to reduce mental events to physical ones shows the pervasiveness of the strong philosophical trends of critical empiricism, associationism, and scientific materialism in the middle of the nineteenth century.

---

[4] La Mettrie's name, incidentally, means "of the hammer," not an inappropriate name for a man who wrote such an iconoclastic work.

# 3

# The Lines
# of Development
# from Science

Of the five scientific trends, two—physiology and quantification—shall be given somewhat closer scrutiny. Developments in biology will be touched on incidentally in various other places in our account, and Charles Darwin's contributions in particular will be discussed in conjunction with consideration of Herbert Spencer in the next chapter. Atomism will be apparent in many formulations and will also, at least implicitly, inevitably be involved in parts of our later discussion of the philosophical trend of associationism. As for the tendency to establish research and training laboratories, not much more can be said than to repeat that it was in the air.

## THE PHYSIOLOGICAL TRENDS

The physiological route to the understanding of psychological phenomena was evident in a variety of fields. There were efforts to find gross structural correlates for different functions, concern with reflex action, study of the nature of nervous conduction and the structure of the nervous system, much interest in the localization of different psychological functions in various parts of the brain, and the attempt to construct a physiological epistemology (in that people tried to account for how we obtain information through the senses, and how this information is passed on from sense organ to brain).

### A Gross Structural Correlate for a Major Function

Important because it showed that clear correlations could be established between physiological and behavioral events was the distinction between the sensory and the motor nerves, published independently by Charles Bell in

21

1811 in England (in a privately printed monograph, of which only 100 copies were made ) and by François Magendie in 1822 in France. They established that the dorsal roots of the spinal cord are sensory, while the ventral are motor. This discovery was hailed as very important, and incidentally also serves to reemphasize the vagaries of history: the same fact had already been pointed out by Eristratus of Alexandria, about 300 B.C., and was reiterated by Galen during the second century A.D. (who, incidentally, disagreed with Aristotle about the locus of the mind: Aristotle placed it in the heart, Galen in the brain). It is curious that the same "important fact" has to be rediscovered periodically.

### Study of the Reflex

In the eighteenth and nineteenth centuries people were concerned with reflex action. Interest in reflexes was no doubt enhanced by René Descartes, whom we shall look at more closely in the next chapter; vestiges of this earlier interest are seen in the twentieth-century emphasis upon conditioning and the tying together of stimuli and responses. The term "reflex" was first used by Astruc in the middle of the eighteenth century. Whytt a little later described detailed experiments with frogs, in which he investigated the role of the spinal cord in reflex action. Some issues concerning reflexes became important in the nineteenth century but have waned since, such as whether reflexes are the unconscious aspect of behavior or whether voluntary work and action are nonreflexive. Although there was still some concern with the voluntary-involuntary question in the first half of the twentieth century, one encounters discussions about it much less nowadays.

### Nervous Conduction

Then there was the investigation of the electrical nature of nerve impulses. Galvani found that a frog's leg would twitch when touched by two different metals, so he postulated the existence of animal electricity. The German physiologist DuBois-Reymond, a contemporary of the great Hermann von Helmholtz, published a book, *On Animal Electricity,* which summarized this area, and moved the phenomena out of the domain of mysticism and into the realm of materialistic science.

Although Johannes Müller said in 1844 that the speed of the nervous impulse was too rapid to be measured, his student Helmholtz in 1850 did measure it with an ingenious experiment. He measured the time interval between stimulus and muscle twitch as a function of how far from the muscle the nerve was stimulated and, by subtraction, came up with a remarkably slow speed, which was largely corroborated later by much more sophisticated research. A detailed electrical theory of *how* the impulse is propagated was not clearly formulated until early in the twentieth century.

## The Structure and Function of the Nervous System

Intense interest in the nervous system and its building blocks characterized much of the nineteenth century. This work led eventually to Santiago Ramón y Cajal's neuron theory. Previous work on the anatomy of the nervous system, and Cajal's own work in staining microscopic sections of the nervous system, led him to the conclusion that it is made up of separate pieces, the neurons, which are hooked together at synapses. The theory implied an associationistic atomism; the whole, that is the nervous system, can be understood as the sum of its connected parts. Making up the trend which was epitomized by the neuron theory were studies of the anatomy of the neuron, identification of axons, the study of differences between grey and white matter, and work on the speed of the nervous impulse as a function of the diameter of the neural fiber and of its myelinization, that is, whether or not the fiber has a white fatty sheath. The membrane theory maintained that the nerve impulse consists of the breakdown of particular electrical charges.    The absolute and relative refractory phases of firing axons were identified and studied, and the all-or-none law—that an axon either fires with all of its energy or not at all—was formulated a little after the turn of the present century. This made for serious problems, since if all a neuron can do is fire or not fire, how is it possible for the nervous system to transmit information about the strength of a stimulus, or its quality? Encoding of the intensity of the stimulus was later hypothesized to occur in terms of the number of neurons firing, and of the frequency of impulses in each fiber; quality of sensation was mediated by which particular fibers were stimulated— according to the doctrine of specific nerve energies, to which we shall return in a moment.

### Localization of Function

Are particular behavioral or psychological functions localized in particular places in the brain? Opinion swung back and forth like a pendulum on this issue.

At the beginning of the nineteenth century Franz Joseph Gall developed the doctrine of organology, which his pupil Johann Caspar Spurzheim popularized and rechristened phrenology. They studied the anatomy and physiology of the nervous system in general, but concentrated on the brain, with particular interest concerning the possibility of recognizing certain intellectual and moral traits of animals and men by examining the convolutions of the head. The theory of phrenology was based on several interlocking hypotheses. First, each mental function is mediated by some particular part of the brain. Second, if a given function is well developed in a person, then his corresponding neural structure also must be particularly well developed, that is, enlarged. Finally, since the shape of the skull to some extent accommodates the shape of the underlying neural tissue, examination of the bumps of the skull should provide information about the degree of development of the underlying neural structures, and correspondingly of the individual's behavioral characteristics. An ingenious theory, but unfortunately it did not work. Later research showed that one cannot identify specific attributes like amativeness, benevolence, reverence, or cautiousness with the development of certain parts of the brain; furthermore, size of anatomical unit and complexity of function are not necessarily correlated, and unusual size of a particular neural structure need not result in an obliging corresponding dent or bump in the skull.

Pierre Flourens, a distinguished Parisian scientist, about 1820 moved away from the extreme of specific localization of the phrenologists. He used the method of extirpation (surgical removal), studying the relation of loss of brain tissue to changes in behavior, and concluded that the brain acts essentially as a whole, although certain lobes do have fairly specific functions within the totality.

The pendulum swung back toward localized specificity in 1861, when Paul Broca, a French physician, identified a "speech center," by reporting that aphasia, or loss of language skills, was associated with a tumor on the lower left side of the brain of a patient in an insane asylum. This sweeping generalization of a finding on a single case was buttressed later by the work of G. Fritsch and E. Hitzig, two German physiologists, who obtained further evidence of localization of function in soldiers who had sustained brain wounds during the Franco-Prussian War. Fritsch also found that if an area of the living brain is touched along the Rolandic fissure, certain eye or finger movements occur. This laid to rest an earlier dogma that the cortex could not be excited. Fritsch and Hitzig continued with laboratory studies on animals, using cortical excitation and extirpation, after the idea of doing such experiments had come to Fritsch on the battlefield. They established the principle of contralateral representation; that is, that functions of the right half of the body are represented in the left half of the brain, and vice versa. Their extensive studies were reported in a publication in 1870, and the pendulum swung back again from Flourens' antispecificity view, but now to specific movements rather than to the general propensities of the kind the phrenologists had tried to identify.

More recent work, such as that of Shepherd Franz and Karl Lashley, returned more to the Flourens position, with some emphasis both on mass action and on specificity. Gestalt psychologists like Wolfgang Köhler, Kurt

Goldstein, and Martin Scheerer in still more recent years performed work that further supported Lashley's principles of equipotentiality (that parts of the brain have the potential of performing the functions of other parts, if these other parts are damaged) and mass action (that the brain acts as a whole, as an integrated unit). Today's view seems to include both: that the brain acts as a totality but that it also has some degree of specificity, particularly with regard to the simpler functions such as basic sensory experiences and specific movements.

### Specific Nerve and Fiber Energies

The doctrine of specific nerve energies was formulated to account for the fact that we can sense different qualities. Johannes Müller systematized this doctrine in his famous *Handbook of Physiology*, providing detailed evidence for it. He argued that the quality of the sensation must "reside in" the neuron itself. DuBois-Reymond went so far as to speculate that if we cut and cross the visual and auditory nerves, we would hear with our eyes and see with our ears!

Hermann von Helmholtz spoke of not only specific nerve energies, but also specific energies for particular *fibers;* he developed a specific fiber energies theory of vision (the Young-Helmholtz color theory, which postulates three different kinds of retinal sensory cells, some sensitive to red, some to blue, and some to green), and also his resonance theory of pitch perception, which requires several thousand specific fiber energies: each of the transverse fibers of the basilar membrane in the inner ear is considered to resonate to, to be sensitive to, a particular frequency of stimulation.

### Other Work in Sensation

A great deal of other work was also being done on sensation. Late in the seventeenth century the physicist Isaac Newton, in a report to the Royal Society, demonstrated that white light can be broken down prismatically into the colors of the rainbow. About a century after that, the physiologist Young proposed the first three-element theory of color vision, which Helmholtz, as mentioned in the preceding paragraph, developed 50 years later into the influential Young-Helmholtz theory. About a quarter of a century after that, Ewald Hering proposed a different color theory, an opponent-process model, which has come back into prominence in recent years. Other developments in vision included Dalton's 1794 description, already referred to, of red-green color blindness; and in the middle of the seventeenth century the French physiologist Mariotte had described the now well-known phenomena of the blind spot. Wheatstone, a physicist famous for his work in electricity, studied color mixture and stereoscopy early in the nineteenth century; he invented the stereoscope, which was to be much used in research by the experimental psychologists of the latter half of the nineteenth and the first half of the twentieth century. The mechanism of accommodation had also been described by Young and by Helmholtz, by the latter in his monumental *Optics.*

Interest in the senses was not limited to vision. Bell (of the Bell-Magendie Law) described the ear in detail during the early 1800s, paying particular attention to the ossicles. Johannes Müller provided an even more detailed description, and Helmholtz, as already mentioned, proposed the resonance place theory to explain pitch perception. The physicist G. S. Ohm, well known for his contributions in electricity, formulated in 1843 what has since been known as Ohm's acoustic law, arguing that the ear acts as a Fourier analyzer, that is, breaks complex tones down into their component pure tones.

The senses of touch and of kinesthesis were studied by E. H. Weber in his doctoral dissertation, published in Latin in 1834, and made available in a larger German version in a chapter Weber wrote for a handbook of physiology, published in 1846. This work included the background for Fechner's later formulation, which he called Weber's Law:

$$\frac{\Delta I}{I} = k$$

that is, the increment in stimulation, required for a subject to sense that the stimulus has increased, remains some constant fraction of the amount of stimulation already present. This formula was to provide the basis for Fechner's later epoch-making general psychophysical law, to which we shall return in Chapter 5.

Smell had also come in for some attention; Linnaeus (Carl von Linné, a professor at the University of Uppsala, in Sweden ), famous for the Linnaean classificatory system in botany, turned his pigeonholing talents to the analysis of smell as well. Somewhat more recent well-known workers in this field include Hendrik Zwaardemaker with his olfactometer, and Hans Henning, who categorized smells into a prismatic space, and more recent yet, workers like Carl Pfaffmann and others who undertook electrophysiological and chemical research in smell and taste.

The illustrations of the last few pages may serve to show how much ferment there was in that portion of physiology which bordered on psychological issues. The active research interests and methods of early quasi-psychological physiology continued as a major focus of scientific endeavor later among the first self-styled experimental psychologists.

## QUANTIFICATION

About 1800 Immanuel Kant asserted flatly that psychology could never be a science. Science requires measurement and experimentation, he held, and one cannot measure or quantify psychological events, or experiment with them, as one can physical phenomena. Both of these arguments were refuted within the next few decades. Among other landmarks, certain fundamental psychological events were translated into mathematical terms by Herbart, by Weber, and by Fechner; psychophysics was developed to measure mental events; and Ebbinghaus did quantitative experimental work with memory.

### The Personal Equation and Reaction Time

An early development in quantification was the formulation of the "personal equation," a forerunner of the study of reaction time. At the Greenwich observatory in England, at the end of the eighteenth century, the astronomer Maskelyne was working with his assistant Kinnebrook in calibrating ships' clocks against the transit of a star across a hairline in the telescope eyepiece. Kinnebrook reported the star passage 0.8 second later than Maskelyne and therefore, so the story goes, Maskelyne fired him.

The Prussian astronomer Friedrich W. Bessel, at Königsberg, heard about the Greenwich matter, and considered the Maskelyne-Kinnebrook difference as due not only to error or sloppiness, but possibly to natural individual differences. So he started to calibrate himself against his colleagues and against people at other observatories with regard to the timing of stellar transits. In this way he managed to compute "personal equations," so that constants could be added to one astronomer's reported times in order to convert his values into those obtained by another astronomer. That is, a time reported by one observer (say $t_m$ for Maskelyne's report) could be converted into another's (say $t_k$ for Kinnebrook's) by the simple formula:

$$t_k = t_m + 0.8$$

The measurement of reaction time, or "mental chronometry," rose out of the personal equation work. The Dutch physiologist Donders performed some early reaction-time experiments, contrasting simple with complex reaction time, the first involving just the making of a predetermined response to a particular stimulus, while the latter involved discrimination among several stimuli or responses. The increase in the amount of time required for a discriminative as against a simple response was considered a measure of how long the mental process of decision took.

Wundt later developed this subtractive method (subtracting the time it takes for a simple task from the time it takes to perform a more complex one) for measuring various mental operations, based upon the difference that Donders had obtained. One of Wundt's students, Lange, discovered that attention to the response decreases the reaction time relative to how long it takes if one pays attention to the stimulus; this led to the distinction between sensory and muscular reaction time. Another student of Wundt's, Oswald Külpe, argued against the subtractive method, asserting that the entire act is not simply the sum of this sensory plus that decision plus the other response process, but rather must be considered as a whole.

This development occurred about 1900, and, although studies of reaction time continued to be important in the first half of the twentieth century, they declined somewhat from their prominent position in the latter half of the nineteenth. Yet, there are still quite a few theoretical and experimental studies of reaction time, as well as practical applications—as, for example, in the selection of airline pilots and cab drivers.

### Statistics

It did not dawn on the early investigators that there are intraindividual differences in variability, in addition to interindividual constant errors, of the kind studied by Friedrich Bessel. It was Christian Gauss,[1] in his study of the general error distribution, who developed the equation for the normal curve and for various measures of variability. This normal distribution was to play a major role in the later study of individual differences and in the interpretation of mental tests; Adolph Quetelet found that in many instances the normal law applied to biological and social measurements on human beings.

Gauss's description of the normal curve of error early in the nineteenth century also was the beginning of a period of invention of a wide variety of statistical procedures. Statistics developed at about the same time as did experimental psychology, with much work going on during the nineteenth century as well as in the first half of the twentieth. The regression equation and the concept of correlation were devised by Sir Francis Galton, and were developed by Karl Pearson, Charles E. Spearman, and others.

Early in the twentieth century the theory of factor analysis, implicit in some of the work of Spearman and further elaborated by men like L. L. Thurstone, provided methods for reducing huge intercorrelation tables to simpler, conceptually meaningful structures. Statistics as we know them today developed rapidly during the first half of the twentieth century, with the name of R. A. Fisher standing out as a major contributor to what is now considered classical statistics; during the middle of the century there arose a major interest in a whole new series of statistical inferential tools, the nonparametric statistics that do not require the series of assumptions that classical statistics require, and that all too often cannot be met by actual measurements.

---

[1] Some have argued that P. S. de Laplace and A. de Moivre have priority over Gauss in developing the normal law of probability, but the curve is nevertheless most widely known as the Gaussian distribution.

## Mathematical Models

Another trend (which has a long history, in that Euclid first developed it, and it was then used by many philosophers, such as Spinoza) is the mathematico-deductive or hypothetico-deductive approach to theorizing characteristic of Clark Hull in mid-twentieth century psychology—that is, a systematic statement of hypotheses and the rigorous deduction of consequences from them. A closely related chain is the construction of mathematical models of psychological processes. In a way, one can consider Fechner's theory, and certainly Herbart's work, both of which we shall consider in a later chapter, as part of this tradition. The construction of mathematical models came up again as a major movement in the middle of the twentieth century, especially in the form of a proliferation of mathematical models of learning.

# 4

# The Lines
# of Development
# from Philosophy

While the five trends from science left their impress upon the later psychology, the contributions of philosophy to the emerging independent discipline was no less marked. Indeed, until fairly recently psychology was typically taught in departments of philosophy. Although the trends from science largely add up to a collection of facts and discoveries, with empirical investigation and a set of popular research areas dominating the Zeitgeist, those from philosophy are more a series of significant fundamental problems, with various different answers and occasional reformulations of the problems proposed by successive philosophers. Each of the three trends—critical empiricism, associationism, and scientific materialism—had a vigorous separate influence upon psychology, so we shall examine each one briefly in turn.

## CRITICAL EMPIRICISM

Before critical empiricism could flourish, there had to be a change in attitude from that prevailing in the Middle Ages, when writers derived their knowledge from authorities like Aristotle and the Church Fathers. The rise of logic, the acceptance of the idea that one should find out for oneself, the break with authority in science, occurred primarily in the sixteenth century—during the Reformation, when the priests' dicta began to be questioned. If one wanted to know how many teeth a horse has, maybe one should look not in a book but in a horse's mouth, even at the risk of getting one's finger of cherished authoritarian prejudice bitten in the process. The Zeitgeist changed with the discovery of America and the rediscovery of old

Latin and Greek texts, and there were major political events, such as the fall of Constantinople, which demonstrated that the order of things to which man was accustomed was not necessarily permanent nor the best one.

### Early Empiricists

Among the influential thinkers who carried the new spirit of freedom of inquiry into scientific matters were Copernicus, who dared to differ with authority in opposing the geocentric system by proposing that the sun, not the earth, is the center of the universe, and Kepler, who mathematized Copernicus' formulations, using his own and Tycho Brahe's measurements of the movements of the heavenly bodies. In the conceptions of these astronomers, man and the earth were not at the center of everything, the earth was not flat, but round, and the motions of the heavenly bodies were not perfectly circular, but elliptical.

Empirical measurement overrode authority, and disturbed deeply entrenched social mores, beliefs, and traditions. In 1600 Gilbert employed a truly experimental method in the study of magnetism, holding certain variables constant, while varying others systematically. About the same time Galileo was developing an empirical and quantitative approach to mechanics and physics, examining natural phenomena rather than Aristotle or Aquinas in order to achieve an understanding of man's physical environment. Sir Francis Bacon extolled the virtues of an inductive, observational approach to knowledge in his *Novum Organum* (1620), and the British physiologist Harvey published his work on the circulation of blood, heralding the new era of an empirical approach to biology. The application of measurement to physical phenomena was extended to the study of light by Isaac Newton. The break with authority pervaded the Zeitgeist.

The questions central to the concern of the critical empiricists had, however, already been asked by the Greeks. They were curious about what the world is made of and how it is possible for a mere human to obtain knowledge of it. Critical empiricism tries to answer both of these questions, but primarily the second one. It was in response to the first question that the sciences of physics, chemistry, and biology arose, and methods for reliable observation were developed. But in response to the second, the critical empiricists asked: What does man contribute to these things, to the knowledge he experiences? What is the nature of our experience? How does the world of experience relate to the world of physical objects?

One of the most important forms of this question was the nativism-empirism issue—namely Is man born with certain ideas, or does everything have to come into his mind through experience? From Plato down through Descartes, it was believed that man was born with at least some ideas, such as the axioms of geometry; most of the later philosophers tended more to the empirism of Aristotle, holding that man is born without knowledge of specific ideas, but that all of his thoughts develop in some way or another from his experience of the world about him.

### Descartes

Reneé Descartes (1596–1650) was one of the great early figures in this development. He reported that he constantly had trouble getting away to find a quiet place where he could think and work, where he could avoid everyday social life and turmoil. He was a courtier and a soldier, taking part in the Thirty Years' War, but is best known as a philosopher and mathematician. According to his account, on November 10, 1619, while he was in winter quarters on the banks of the Danube, he had a dream which resulted in analytical geometry. The invention of a coordinate space for the translation of algebraic terms into geometrical ones, and vice versa, was a landmark in the history of mathematics.

In his philosophical musings, he was determined to start from the beginning, and to try to find that which he could be certain of *without* recourse to authority. He doubted everything he could possibly doubt. He decided that the only thing which he could be certain of was his doubting; everything else could be a self-deceptive illusion, but he could not doubt the process of doubting itself. Arguing that doubting implies a doubter, he became convinced of his own existence, resulting in the famous statement *cogito ergo sum,* "I think, therefore I am." Having, to his own satisfaction, unquestionably established his own existence, he went on to prove the existence of God and of the real world. In doing so, he tried also to prove that certain ideas, particularly mathematical and religious ones, are innate in man.

Descartes espoused a mind-body dualism much like that of Plato; the body is conceived as material substance ("extended matter"), and the mind as unextended substance ("thinking matter"). Descartes was convinced that mind and body interact; he tentatively chose the pineal gland at the base of the brain as the probable locus of this interaction, but was not fully satisfied with this formulation. The body itself is a machine, like any physical body including stars and stones (a belief that also has the flavor of scientific materialism); man's soul, on the other hand, is not a machine. Animals are bodies without souls, and are therefore automata, or machines. Man, in addition to his animal body, has "l'âme"—a soul or a mind, the unextended substance which distinguishes him from the animals. The soul perceives, wills, and has built-in ideas such as the axioms of geometry or of algebra (like multiplication and addition) and the idea of God; many ideas also come from experience.

Descartes, then, held a somewhat nativistic view, believed in an interactive mind-body dualism, and maintained a scientific materialism, at least as far as man's body and animals were concerned.

### Hobbes

Thomas Hobbes (1588–1679) saw man's mind as active, and sought to analyze the dynamics of this activity. The springs of action, Hobbes held, are pleasure and pain, a hedonistic view already propounded by some Greek philosophers and also held by his contemporary, Descartes. Descartes and Hobbes argued that love is an emotion associated with positive affect, with pleasure, while hate is associated with unpleasure; we do what we do because we try to achieve pleasure and avoid pain. These ideas were later to be picked up by Jeremy Bentham and the rational economists, who tried to account for the behavior of economic man in terms of simple pleasure and pain; they also form the conceptual core of much of psychoanalysis and of several twentieth-century learning theories, such as those of Edward Thorndike and Clark Hull.

Hobbes lived during a time of revolution and political unrest; in 1588, the year of his birth, the Spanish Armada was destroyed, and England became the chief seapower and colonizer. Hobbes, a staunch Royalist, was profoundly troubled by the beheading of Charles I in 1648; he thought deeply and personally about political issues. His major work in political science, published in 1651, entitled *Leviathan,* supported the natural right of kings; in this book he undertook analyses which make it possible to consider him the father of social psychology: What are the conditions giving rise to chaos, to revolution, and to social change? (Other contenders for this paternity could include Machiavelli and Sir Thomas More, predecessors of Hobbes, both of whom had also attempted dispassionate analyses of political behavior.)

Like Machiavelli and many other pessimistic philosophers before and since, Hobbes assumed that man's basic nature is evil: he is motivated by thirst, fear, hunger, self-honor. The social order, an uneasy contract among men, is needed if men are to live at peace with each other. Such ideas, which have a venerable origin, were also to be important much later, as in Freud's concept of the fundamentally self-seeking nature of man.

### Spinoza

Benedict Spinoza's (1632–1677) philosophy was written in far more logical, geometrical form, using axioms and theorems, than were the works of Descartes or Hobbes. An expert lens grinder by trade, he wrote on epistemology and ethics, but is perhaps best known for his proposed solution of the mind-body problem. He developed double-aspect monism, a position which holds that mind and body are but two different aspects of the same unitary basic underlying substance—they are like the two sides of a coin.

### Locke

John Locke (1632–1704), an influential British philosopher, was primarily a politician; when the Earl of Shaftesbury was prime minister, Locke served as his secretary. In 1690 Locke published his *Essay Concerning Human Understanding*. This book, it is interesting to note, was the belated product of an inquiry that Locke had made in preparation for a paper that he had agreed to present at an informal evening discussion club of which he was a member. The work represents a realistic, matter-of-fact, commonsense examination of the bedrock question of critical empiricism: How do we obtain knowledge?

For Locke, the *idea* is the fundamental unit or element of mind. The elements are tied together in groups; hence we need a principle of association. Locke was the first to use this particular term, in a later edition of his book. The ideas which are associated may be simple or compound. No idea is innate; *all* ideas come from experience (or from reflection—a process in which the mind looks back into itself); like Aristotle, then, Locke believed that at birth the mind is a clean slate—even the axioms of geometry and the idea of God come solely through sensation and reflection.

Locke also distinguished between primary and secondary qualities of perceptions. The primary correspond directly to characteristics of the real object: solidity, figure, motion, number, shape, and weight. Secondary qualities are aroused in us by the powers of the object; they do not resemble the object or represent the properties of the object: color, sound, and taste. Thus the object reflects certain wavelengths of light, but the color quality as such is not in the object itself, but "in us."

Locke, then, was primarily an empirist, and interested not so much in what people do as in the nature of mind. This emphasis on the contents of the mind makes Locke a forerunner of twentieth-century structuralism in psychology; by contrast, Hobbes, with his emphasis on the activity of mind, can be seen as a forerunner of nineteenth-century act psychology and twentieth-century functionalism.

Aside from his contributions in philosophy and aside from his being secretary to a prime minister, Locke was also a highly influential political theorist: his treatise on government had a profound impact on the United States Constitution.

### Leibnitz

Gottfried Wilhelm Leibnitz (1646–1716), a contemporary of Locke and of Newton, was a philosopher, a world traveler, and a mathematician. Independently of Newton, and at about the same time, he conceived the calculus. A bitter and useless squabble arose among Newton's and Leibnitz' friends about priority; nowadays we still use the symbols Leibnitz invented.

In his most important philosophical work, the *Monadology,* Leibnitz held that the world is made up of independent monads. The monads are self-sufficient atoms that do not interact, but each contains its entire past and future. In contrast to Locke, for Leibnitz all knowledge is therefore innate. But if all monads are "windowless," have no access to the "outside," do not influence other monads nor are influenced by them, why do monads—like the mind and the body—*seem* to interact? How are they coordinated? Leibnitz' answer, which avoids the problem of a material substance being affected by or affecting an immaterial substance, is the concept of preestablished harmony, or psychophysical parallelism. Monads act as though they are synchronous clocks, all showing the same time, but not affecting each other. It is God who synchronizes the clocks of psychophysical parallelism for the monads, and the mutual influence among monads is only apparent.

In Leibnitz' conception, the mind monad is active; it has degrees of clarity and degrees of consciousness. His analysis made a critical distinction between sensation and higher-level perceptual processes. There are *petites perceptions,* which are in a sense subthreshold, and correspond to sensation; at a higher level of clarity, there is apperception, resulting in suprathreshold awareness. Clear perceptions are apperceptions, while the least clear ones are unnoticed sensations below the threshold of awareness. Enough sensations combined may result in an apperception, as a single pebble moving on the beach may not be heard, but a large group of moving pebbles makes a clearly audible sound. This summative atomism was also characteristic of many later writers on sensation and perception, such as James Mill, Wilhelm Wundt, and E. B. Titchener.

### Berkeley

George Berkeley (1685–1753) was an Irish theologian and philosopher. For many years he was bishop of Cloyne, and traveled widely in the New World, including traveling in Rhode Island. He went to Bermuda with the hope of establishing a university there; he was unsuccessful, but a city in California, still important on the educational scene, is named after him. Later in his life he inherited some money, left his bishopric, and went to Oxford, where he spent his time philosophizing and speculating. When he was in his early twenties, he wrote two works that were to have a profound impact on later philosophy and especially on critical empiricism : *The New Theory of Vision* in 1709, and *Principles of Human Knowledge* in 1710.

For Berkeley, mind is the immediate reality (which is reminiscent of Descartes' *cogito ergo sum*): *esse est percipi*—to be is to be perceived; to be perceived is to be. The question is not how mind affects matter (as in Descartes) or how matter generates mind (as in Locke), but how mind generates matter, since mind is the basic given. This is the philosophy of idealism, leading ultimately to solipsism (from *solo ipse,* "only the self"—the belief that the only reality is myself and that of which I am aware). How can I know that there really is something outside my mind causing and corresponding to my perceptions? The only thing that I can be sure of is that I have various experiences—it is impossible to escape the solipsistic trap that ultimately all we can know is our own experience.

But Berkeley did try to escape solipsism, by way of the concept of a perfect God. Since a God who allows us to deceive ourselves is less perfect than one who would not permit such deception, our experience must correspond to the "real world out there." In effect, God put the real world out there so as to correspond to our experience, simply because God is good. So Berkeley did, in a sense, believe in the existence of the outside world, although he made it a logical derivation, contingent upon God's beneficence.

Berkeley also distinguished between perception and imagination by classifying our ideas about the world; vivid ones we call perceptions, while less vivid ones are imaginations. But Locke's distinction between primary and secondary ideas dissolves in Berkeley's idealism; there are no such things as primary qualities, since everything depends on the mind.

The chief contribution of Berkeley's *New Theory of Vision* was a carefully worked-out empiristic approach to perception. The visual perception of objects and of distance is based on experience, is learned by association, with tactual-kinesthetic sensations forming the basis of the learning. Berkeley provided a remarkably modern summary of the cues for the perception of distance. The primary cues, according to Berkeley, are accommodation, convergence, and blurring; he also described what have been considered the secondary cues for distance perception, like superposition, perspective, and relative size. Experience, said Berkeley, makes it possible for us to interpret such cues in terms of the perceived distance of visual objects.

### Hume

David Hume (1711–1776) stated Berkeley's idealistic monism even more consistently, persuasively and convincingly, without bringing in God to support a conviction about the existence of a real physical world. A Scottish philosopher and historian (writing, among other things, a major history of England), he held various political positions. Hume was a restless person, a perfectionist, and several writers have conjectured that he was held back by his own standards of achievement. (At one point his internal standards kept him from trying to achieve only moderate scholastic success and so immobilized him that he flunked out of school, and in his later youth he could not seem to do anything right; his mother despaired that he would ever be able to get a job and be continuously gainfully employed.) But somehow he managed, and left a major impact on Western thought. His important works include *Treatise on Human Nature,* published when he was 28, and *Inquiry Concerning the Human Understanding,* his most significant philosophical work, published when he was 38.

Mind, Hume argued, knows only its own processes. This led him to doubt the existence of external reality, of anything (including God) outside his own mind. Hume's skepticism about reality extended even to the existence of self—the ego is, fundamentally, nothing more than a collection of ideas, a view that might be called nothing-but atomistic empiricism. His acceptance of Berkeleyan solipsism was complete, in that he did not feel compelled to bring in God to try to justify the existence of a real world. Apparently Hume did not enjoy the skepticism to which his reasoning had brought him, but he was intellectually honest enough to admit that he did not know how to pull himself out of it.

Hume's celebrated analysis of cause and effect is a consequence of his general skepticism: How can we know that there really is a necessary connection between them? The "necessary connection" could easily be just a perceptual illusion produced by the repeated contiguity in time and space of certain events. Hume also followed Berkeley in distinguishing between impressions (sensations and perceptions) and images (which are faint copies of the impressions); the contents of the mind include simple and complex ideas, the latter formed out of simple ones by association.

### Kant

Immanuel Kant (1724–1804), professor of philosophy at Königsberg, an old town in East Prussia, bears a name that is almost synonymous for students of philosophy with the paradoxical combination of clarity, obscurity, pedantry, and intelligence. Strictly an academic, he epitomized the image of the Herr Professor, being interested solely in matters of the mind. He never traveled far from Königsberg, although he was interested in many things, including geography, astronomy, pacifism, and religion. Among his influential philosophical treatises is the *Critique of Pure Reason,* on which he worked for about ten years, and which appeared in 1781. Kant says that he wrote it because Hume's skepticism had "roused him from his dogmatic slumbers."

In this work, Kant compared himself to Copernicus, reversing the order of things: our perceptions, he says, do not give us our concepts, but our percepts are given to us according to our concepts—according to our inborn ways of perceiving the world. These inborn molds, filters, or "categories," as Kant called them, include cause and effect, time and space; we cannot perceive the world in other than causal, spatial, and temporal terms. Thus the mind makes us perceive the world according to certain innate principles or categories; the categories are responsible for the organization and structure of our perceptions. (Kant's statement that the mind is responsible for the organization of perception is a clear anticipation of later gestalt theory.) A real world does, said Kant, exist—the world of noumena, or things-in-themselves—but we can never be directly aware of it without the interposition of the filter of our categories.

### Critical Empiricism After Kant

The immediate post-Kantian philosophers pointed to the absurdity of belief in Kant's noumena, the real world which is by definition unknowable, and the fundamental epistemological question of the nature—and existence—of an extrasubjective world has remained thorny ever since. Later in the nineteenth century, and carrying over into the twentieth, there developed the "positivistic" movement, which tried to analyze experience with the aim of discovering that which we could be positive of, but a genuinely satisfactory answer has not been achieved.

The critical empiricist tradition was responsible for the continued concern with methodology in nineteenth- and twentieth-century psychology. The research spirit, which persistently asks, What do we *really* know, what can we conclude, how can we be reasonably sure? gave rise to such movements as operationism in the twentieth century, and to the concern with objectivity and "the scientific method," which had their roots in the philosophical thought of critical empiricism.

### ASSOCIATIONISM

The attempt to explain a complex whole as a concatenation of units, elements, or atoms hooked together in specifiable ways was made by the Greeks, and continued to be very popular through the ages, down to the present. Aristotle had stated his three laws of association: contiguity, similarity, and contrast; much later Locke, as we mentioned a few pages earlier, reintroduced the concept of association, and Berkeley and Hume made extensive use of it. The development of associationism in England and Scotland profoundly affected modern psychology; it explained complex mental phenomena in terms of the hooking up of elements. Edward L. Thorndike called his early twentieth-century psychology "connectionism," and a perusal of the contents of, for example, the *Journal of Experimental Psychology* or the *Journal of Verbal Learning and Verbal Behavior* in recent years will show that many experiments are still carried out in this area.

### Hartley

*Hume 1711–1776*

The clear statements of David Hartley (1705–1757) helped reestablish the doctrine of associationism in modern Western philosophy. In his work *Some Observations on Man,* he presented what could be considered an early physiological psychology of mental life; a core idea in it was that the physiological correlates of ideas become associated in the brain. Hartley argued that stimuli produce vibrations in nerves, and sensations are the result of the vibrations; these vibrations do not stop suddenly but continue, after cessation of the stimulus, in a weaker form. He called the residues of vibrations "vibratiuncles"; they are responsible for afterimages and for memory, and can be associated by contiguity. Hartley's physiological speculations bear a striking similarity to parts of the later, more sophisticated theory of D. O. Hebb, so influential around the middle of the twentieth century. Hebb's use of the concept of reverberating neural circuits, in his theory, is closely analogous to Hartley's use of the concept of vibratiuncles.

Hartley's laws of association include repetition as well as contiguity, and he used them much as his contemporary Hume did. He also argued that simple associations get compounded into clusters or complex ideas, so that the idea of an apple, for example, is a complex compound of many associated elements. Many much more recent views such as those of Clark Hull or Kenneth Spence were quite similar to those of Hartley, in spite of Karl Lashley's warning early in the present century that explanations in terms of reflex arcs and chains of associated neurons are doomed to failure because they are too static. Perhaps the idea holds on so tenaciously because it is so beautifully simple. The spirit of Hartley is still very much alive in contemporary associationism, in the conditioning approach, in the research field of verbal learning, and in some physiological attempts to explain behavior.

### The Scottish School

The Scottish school, which flourished during the eighteenth century, further developed associationism. Thomas Brown, who preferred the term "suggestion" to the term "association" (one idea may *suggest* another), specified some conditions for association in addition to contiguity and repetition: liveliness, intensity, and recency, among others. In the Scottish school were also Thomas Reid and Dugald Stewart, the latter the teacher of James Mill; both supported the associationist position, but did not add any major systematic changes. It was Reid who formulated the twenty-odd powers of the mind which formed the basis of Gall's classification of the faculties. Sir William Hamilton added the important concept of redintegration: if one element in a large associative compound stored in one's memory is reactivated, one may become conscious of the entire compound again, as when a distinctive smell reminds you of an earlier experience, bringing it back into consciousness in vivid detail.

### The Mills

According to several historians of psychology, James Mill (1773–1836) represents the culmination of the philosophy of associationism. A civil servant in India, and a distinguished historian who wrote a major history of India, he published in 1829 *An Analysis of the Phenomena of the Human Mind.* He was a strict elementist, conceiving of the mind as constituted solely of sensations and ideas, the latter classified as simple or complex, the complex being compounds of simple ideas. There is only one basic principle of association: contiguity—ideas about events occurring at the same time tend to be associated (a view to be developed again in detail, in a slightly different version, by E. R. Guthrie during the twentieth century). Any mental whole, for Mill, is the sum total of the compounded ideas or elements.

James Mill's son, John Stuart Mill (1806–1873) provided a major new departure for the associationist doctrine in his contention that an associative compound may have properties different from those of its component parts. Individually tutored by his father in his early years, he later was a clerk in the India House and a member of Parliament in the House of Commons. Although he wrote no books on psychology, he did write influential treatises in such areas as logic, political science, liberty, utilitarianism, and woman sufferage.

Convinced like his father that association is the primary law of mind, John Stuart Mill wrote a detailed commentary on his father's work, in the form of lengthy footnotes. He preferred the term "mental chemistry" for the compounding of ideas, and argued that the compound of several elements can yield something entirely new—as, for example, the wetness of water is not deducible from the properties of the elements composing it. The compounds often act like new units, or new elements with new properties. Ideas melt and coalesce with each other, forming new wholes.

J. S. Mill also made some contributions to critical empiricism: he argued that matter is the permanent possibilities of sensation; that exists which can potentially be perceived. Perception, he held, includes a belief in the real existence of the object.

## Spencer and Darwin

Herbert Spencer (1820–1903) was trained as an engineer; early in his career he became a permanent invalid, so he decided to devote his time to writing treatises about all of the sciences, including sociology, political science, and psychology. In 1855 there appeared his two-volume *Principles of Psychology.* The work included the new idea of evolutionary associationism: associations which are often repeated in the lifetime of the individual or in the race will be transmitted to the offspring as an evolutionary instinct. This is how instincts like the web-spinning of the spider or the nest-building of birds arise; instincts are inherited concatenations of reflexes. His work anticipated, and his later thinking was influenced by, Darwin's *Origin of Species* (1859).

The breadth of Spencer's thought (which went far beyond a pure, limited associationism) is exemplified by his espousal, in his *Principles of Psychology,* of a double-aspect monism much like Spinoza's; he also developed a hedonistic account of motivation. The book included, further, discussions of feelings, and of the elements of mind; in a section on education he maintained that the aim of schooling is to facilitate adjustment to one's environment: "Life is a continual adjustment of internal to external circumstances." An emphasis upon adjustment has been particularly characteristic of the functionalist American psychology of the first half of the twentieth century; the view is still prevalent in the current Zeitgeist.

Evolutionary thinking affected the associationist traditions in the direct form inherent in Spencer's evolutionary associationist doctrine of instinct, and also became the fundamental hedonistic concept in Thorndike's law of effect and Hull's principle of reinforcement. Darwin's emphasis on the survival of the species that "works," that fits its surrounding, has a close parallel in the modern learning theorist's principle that those responses in an organism's repertoire will survive which "work" in the sense of satisfying needs, but those which do not, or which lead to annoyance or pain, will drop out, as Thorndike and Hull held.

Charles Darwin (1809–1882) is important in the history of psychology primarily because of his vast and detailed *Origin of Species* (1859), in which he supported with massive data his major principle of evolution: the survival of the fit, that is, of those organisms that are well suited to their ecological circumstances. (Alfred Russell Wallace proposed a similar theory in a brief paper at about the same time, but did not present the huge wealth of data in support of it which Darwin had amassed.) Darwin also wrote a more psychological book, *The Expression of Emotion in Man and Animal.* In this work he pointed out that evolution occurs not only in morphology but also in behavior, including the expression of emotion; examples of evolutionary vestiges include the baring of teeth in dogs before they fight, which still has some utility, as against the clenching of the teeth in an angry human, where the adjustive function of preparing to bite is, at least in modern civilized society, much less clear. The balling of the fist in anger may also be a vestige of an earlier time when such a response was more clearly useful.

### Bain

A professor of philosophy at the University of Aberdeen in Scotland, Alexander Bain (1818–1903) wrote the first systematic textbook of psychology in English. The book has a distinctly modern outline, and was the first work on psychology to begin with a chapter on neurology. As a whole, the work is more systematic than that written by Spencer at about the same time. Bain's work was published in two parts: in 1855 Part One, *The Senses and the Intellect;* in 1859 Part Two *The Emotions and the Will*—the will being identified by Bain with the spontaneous activity of the nervous system. The work was one of the first to include a chapter on habit. His chapter on association included two laws—contiguity and similarity—and also a rudimentary statement of what was later, in Thorndike's hands, to become the law of effect: behavior occurs according to trial and error, with chance movements, from among which the successful ones are selected.

It is also of interest to note that in 1872 Bain published *Mind and Body,* the first text devoted to this topic; he himself espoused a psychophysical parallelist position, because he felt that interactionism is incompatible with the notions of conservation of energy. In 1876 he founded the first psychological journal, *Mind,* which was to be a major outlet for influential philosophical and psychological works, including a paper by Darwin on education and childhood training.

## SCIENTIFIC MATERIALISM

Scientific materialism is the belief that the phenomena of mind and behavior are ultimately describable in the concepts of the mathematical and physical sciences. Proponents of this view maintain that scientific explanations must avoid unobservable, supernatural forces. Opposite to scientific materialism are animism and vitalism. Animism holds that spirits inhabit inanimate things; it leads to concern with such matters as souls, spirits, reincarnation. Vitalism, as espoused by the biologists Johannes Müller and Hans Driesch and by the philosopher Henri Bergson, with his concept of the élan vital, holds that living beings do what they do because of the vital spirit within them, a spirit that transcends their physical characteristics; a nonmaterial active agent determines the behavior of living things.

### French Materialism

Scientific materialism grew out of French philosophical materialism; some of Hobbes' mechanistic ideas can also be seen as forerunners of later scientific materialism. Descartes too had already taught that animals are automata; and Julien de La Mettrie, about a century later, made the same statement as Descartes, but claimed that it held of human beings as well as of animals: men too are at bottom automata. His *L'Homme machine,* which appeared in 1748, was the first attempt to devote a whole book to the objective, materialistic, naturalistic description of behavior. One might, in a sense, consider La Mettrie the first behaviorist.

A short time after La Mettrie, Etienne de Condillac, in his *Treatise on Sensations,* carried on the argument that man's behavior can be explained mechanically, materialistically. If one endows a marble statue with only the sense of smell, he proposed, one can generate the entire gamut of mental processes in it. Although the statue will then have a mind, Condillac argued, it will have no soul. The Swiss philosopher, Charles Bonnet, wrote a book with a similar theme, but endowed his statue with the sense of sight and with nerves.

Pierre Cabanis, a French physician who took part in the French Revolution, in 1789 raised the question (appropriate to the Ortgeist because of the wide use of the guillotine) of whether beheaded people still sense and think. He studied the reflexes of severed heads and bodies, and his researches convinced him that consciousness is the function of the brain, much as digestion is the function of the stomach. But once the body is separated from the head, the head is no longer conscious. Thus the scientific materialistic answer to the question of whether beheaded people still sense and think was, according to Cabanis, No.

### British Materialism

The British versions of scientific materialism were not as extreme and outspoken as those of the French, but the tendency was there nevertheless. Scientific materialism came into British writings, as it were, somewhat casually. W. Harvey, about a century before Descartes, had written in Latin on the motion of the heart and the blood, implicitly describing these functions as purely mechanical and hydraulic; vital spirits or animal spirits had no place in his account. In 1677 F. Glisson, a noted philosopher-physician in England, pointed to the importance of an experiment by the Dutchman J. Swammerdam, in which it was demonstrated that the contraction of muscles is not due to their being entered and expanded by mysterious animal spirits. If a muscle is immersed in water, then contracted, this does not raise the level of the water. This elegant, simple experiment provided a direct disproof of the Cartesian notion that the contraction of muscles is due to the flowing in of substantial animal spirits. We earlier touched on the researches of Robert Whytt, who demonstrated in the middle of the eighteenth century that reflexes in frogs are due to specific stimulation, and that no animistic or vital force is required to explain their occurrence. At about the same time, David Hartley was trying to reduce mental processes to his physiological speculations concerning vibrations and vibratiuncles, which he conceived of as strictly natural, material events within the nervous system.

### German Materialism

German thinkers like Leibnitz and Kant tended toward idealism in philosophy, but toward scientific materialism (with some reservations) in science (thus Johannes Müller, for example, was a leading biological and physiological scientist, but held a vitalist position). Wöhler's synthesis of urea in 1828, already referred to several times, demonstrated that the production of organic compounds does not depend upon the presence of a living body; his synthesis destroyed vitalism in chemistry.

Perhaps the most dramatic declaration of scientific materialism was made by four of Johannes Müller's students, all in their twenties at the time, in 1842. The manifesto was written by DuBois-Reymond in collaboration with the physiologist Ernst Brücke; soon after, Hermann von Helmholtz and Karl Ludwig joined them, and legend has it that each signed it with his own blood. Although no one objected to scientific materialism in the physical sciences, the closer that one came to psychology, the greater the general opposition seemed to be, perhaps mainly on religious and ethical grounds. DuBois wrote, "Brücke and I pledged a solemn oath to put into effect this truth: no forces other than the common physical-chemical ones are active within the organism. In those cases which cannot at the time be explained by these forces one has either to find the specific way or form of their action by means of the physical-mathematical methods or to assume new forces equal in dignity to the chemical-physical forces inherent in matter, reducible to the forces of attraction and repulsion."

### Later Materialism

Later in the nineteenth century and early in the twentieth, partly as an outgrowth of the Darwinian revolution, biological workers like George John Romanes, C. Lloyd Morgan, John Lubbock, and Jacques Loeb provided detailed mechanical descriptions of animal behavior. In 1890 Loeb reported some of his work on the tropisms, or specific, directed mechanical movements of animals—and plants—as a function of stimulation; the tropistic view, growing out of German materialism, was an explicit return to Descartes' conception of organisms as automata. Russian reflexology, too, in the nineteenth and early twentieth century, with contributors like Sechenov, Bekhterev, and Pavlov, had a profound effect upon the growth of American behaviorism. It will be considered in greater detail in Chapter 12, when we summarize the antecedents of behaviorism.

Perhaps best known as an extension of the DuBois statement is Lloyd Morgan's version of the law of parsimony, later referred to as "Lloyd Morgan's Canon: " "In no case may we interpret an action as the outcome of the exercise of a higher physical faculty, if it can be interpreted as the outcome of the exercise of one which stands lower in the psychological scale." In the twentieth century John B. Watson, and especially B. F. Skinner, were exemplars of the thoroughgoing application of scientific materialism to all behavior of all organisms, including man.

## SUMMARY OF PART I

Although the origins of many of the trends culminating in the experimental psychology of 1860 and beyond can be seen in Greek and pre-Renaissance thought, it is primarily the history of ideas since the Renaissance which casts light upon the academic and intellectual Ortgeist and Zeitgeist of mid-nineteenth century Europe, where experimental psychology was born.

Five major lines of development from science contributed to the birth of experimental psychology about 1860. In *physiology,* there were the rediscovery of the anatomical distinction between sensory and motor nerves, the study of the electrical nature of the nerve impulse, anatomical and functional studies culminating in the neuron theory, the controversy concerning the localization of functions in the brain, the doctrine of specific nerve energies, and extensive research in sensation. *Biology* contributed the careful study of morphology and, to a lesser extent, behavior; the most important influence from biology was the concept of evolution. *Atomism* was a prevalent and useful approach in chemistry and in other fields, and therefore many people tried to be atomistic in the analysis of mental phenomena. The desirability of *quantification* was very much in the Zeitgeist; study of the personal equation led to mental chronometry and the study of reaction time; statistical tools for the description of a wide variety of phenomena were developed, and the psychophysical methods grew out of the attempt to quantify mental events. Finally, there was a strong tendency toward the *establishment of* formal university research and training *laboratories,* particularly in chemistry.

Three major trends in philosophy influenced the newly developing science of psychology. *Critical empiricism,* with roots in Greek and Renaissance thought, and carried on by the new philosophers—among whom Descartes, Locke, Berkeley, Hume, and Kant stand out—asked the important question of how one can acquire knowledge. *Associationism,* begun by Aristotle, and taken over particularly by the British philosophers of the eighteenth and nineteenth centuries, attempted to explain how ideas hang together. *Scientific materialism* had its origins in Descartes, was picked up in particular by French philosophers, but was also contributed to by British and German thinkers: one of its chief tenets is that mind and behavior are part of the natural world, and can be described and studied just as scientifically and materialistically as any other phenomena.

It was, then, out of scientific developments in physiology and biology, the establishment of laboratories, and the tendency toward quantified atomistic thinking, as well as the philosophical views of associationism, critical empiricism, and scientific materialism, that the new science of experimental psychology arose.

# PART II

# The Rise
# of Experimental
# Psychology

# 5

# Wundt's
# Immediate Predecessors

Whether we point to the year 1879, in which Wilhelm Wundt later said he had first performed new research in the first laboratory of experimental psychology, or choose 1860, the year of publication of Fechner's *Elements of Psychophysics,* or select still some other arbitrary date, like the year 1875, when Wundt at Leipzig (and also James at Harvard) received space for a demonstration laboratory for psychology, clearly it was during the latter half of the nineteenth century in Germany that experimental psychology achieved its status as an independent science. The new discipline manifested the eight trends we considered in Part I: it was influenced by the five developments in science (physiology and biology, quantification and atomism, and the founding of laboratories) and the three in philosophy (associationism, critical empiricism, and scientific materialism).

Fechner may have been the herald of the new psychology, but Wundt was its founder. Accordingly, Part II is organized primarily around Wundt. First we shall characterize German psychology just before his time, to provide context and further background. Then we shall consider Wundt and his system in some detail, and thereafter some other figures who were prominent in late nineteenth-century psychology. Part II ends with a glance at American psychology, for by the early twentieth century psychology's center of gravity had shifted from Germany to the United States.

## SOME GERMAN CONTRIBUTORS BEFORE WUNDT

The German Zeitgeist in the age of Wundt was an Ortgeist; it was local to Germany and still characterized much of German psychology during the twentieth century. The intellectual climate was academic, with a ponderous terminology and many heavy, serious, hard-to-read tomes; many of these works were very formal and appear pedantic or even picayune to the modern reader. The Ortgeist was scientific, with an emphasis upon rigid experimentation, and systematic, with explicitly stated, thorough theoretical formulations. Paradoxically, mysticism was in the air at the same time, particularly on the fringes of psychology, in concerns with God, with social behavior, and with the soul. Romanticism was locking horns with classicism, and there was much interest in other languages and cultures, particularly exotic oriental ones. The great literary figure Goethe exemplified this fascination with folk culture and with emotional expression. It is perhaps no accident that psychology was, somewhat romantically, concerned not with behavior, but with experience (in contrast with the American Ortgeist, particularly the later behaviorism, with its extreme emphasis on the "objective"); but German psychology was also physiological, largely under the influence of the scientific trends characterized in Chapter 3.

### Wolff

This spirit had been developing over a long period. Leibnitz, whom we considered in Chapter 4 under the heading "Critical Empiricism," was a major early figure in this development. His approach influenced another eighteenth-century philosopher, Christian von Wolff (1679–1754). A contemporary of Hume, Wolff published two major, formidable treatises: *Empirical Psychology* in 1734 and *Rational Psychology* in 1754. In these volumes, Wolff expounded and popularized Leibnitz. Adopting a psychophysical parallelist view of the mind-body relation, Wolff also attempted a detailed explanation of human mental events in terms of faculties; he proposed a set of faculties for knowing, remembering, imagining, sensing, understanding, reasoning, loving, and so forth. This faculty psychology was to be used later so ingeniously by the phrenologists. In his discussion of the will, Wolff argued that feelings of pleasure and pain determine behavior, carrying on and strengthening the hedonist tradition, which was already evident in Descartes and Hobbes and which was to culminate in the law of effect of Thorndike and the law of reinforcement of Hull. Wolff was the first writer to use the word "psychology" in the title of a monograph[1].

### Herbart

A major pre-Wundtian figure was Johann Friedrich Herbart (1776–1841), philosopher, psychologist, and, according to some, the first educational psychologist; one can also make a case for him as the first mathematical

---

[1] The first use of the word "psychology" as such was apparently by Martin Luther's linguistic consultant, Philip Melanchthon—whose last name, incidentally, as was the custom of the day, was rendered into Greek in his writings; his real name, it seems, was Schwarzerd—or "black earth."

psychologist. Even though he contradicted Kant concerning the possibility of a science of psychology, by developing a sophisticated mathematical approach to psychology, he succeeded Kant as professor of philosophy at Königsberg. That Herbart was offered the chair at Königsberg was apparently no accident, since the university was at the time famous for mathematics, with such renowned men as the mathematician-logician Euler on its faculty. After Königsberg, Herbart went to Göttingen, also well known for its contributions to mathematics.

Herbart published his *Textbook of Psychology* in 1816, and *Psychology as Science* in 1821. It was in the second book that Herbart gave what he considered his answer to Kant; he showed that psychology could be quantitative. Already in the *Textbook,* he maintained that psychology must be based on experience, that is, it must be empirical; further, it should and can be mathematical. However, he held that it could be neither physiological nor experimental, because physiological concerns and experimental techniques tend to fractionate, and one must deal with the mind as a whole. This conception of the mind as organized and unitary is similar to gestalt ideas that were to emerge a century later.

According to Herbart, ideas in the mind are dynamic; they possess energy in that they attract or repel one another. The ideas are constantly at war; they struggle with each other to win a place in consciousness. Ideas are thus never really forgotten; they are just pushed below the threshold or limen of consciousness by competing ideas.

Herbart's formulation thus makes explicit use of the concept of the unconscious and of repression, which were to play such a major role in Freud's later theorizing; it also anticipates some aspects of Kurt Lewin's dynamic psychology. The ideas strive to rise into consciousness, but can do so only when the ideas already in consciousness—that is, what Herbart called the "apperceptive mass"—are receptive to that idea. The new ideas fuse with the apperceptive mass; what one learns, therefore, depends to a large extent on what one already knows, and on the immediate mental set. The function of attention is to produce an appropriate apperceptive mass, making ideas easier to consider, easier to apperceive. Herbart quantified his theories of apperception, the limen of consciousness, the activity of ideas, and their fusion in a manner clearly anticipating some of today's mathematical models approaches.

Basing his pedagogy upon his psychology, Herbart argued in his educational prescriptions that the teacher, in planning his lesson, should follow five steps: (1) Review previous material. (2) Prepare for what is to come next—the purpose of this is to induce an appropriate apperceptive mass. (3) When the mind is in the right receptive state—and only then—present the new material. (4) Relate the new material to what came before. And, finally, (5) Look forward, showing applications of the new material and also introducing what will come next. Many teachers today still use some variant of this teaching technique, and it is considered by many to be very effective.

### J. Müller and Weber

Two physiologists, both mentioned before, also contributed substantially to the rise of experimental psychology: Johannes Müller and E. H. Weber. Müller's influential *Handbook of Physiology* included detailed discussions of depth perception and sensation, and presented a full statement of the doctrine of specific nerve energies. Weber did quantitative work in a number of sensory modalities, studied the two-point threshold (finding that there were major differences among various parts of the body in how far apart two points touched simultaneously had to be, in order for a person to tell that they were two and not just one), and concentrated upon the just noticeable difference (that is, how much does a stimulus have to be changed for a person to notice that it has changed): the *jnd* (or just noticeable difference) work resulted in the generalization that Fechner later called Weber's Law (discussed later in the present chapter under "Fechner's Law").

### Lotze

Another godfather of the new psychology was the philosopher-psychologist Hermann Lotze (1817–1881), a patron of the experimental psychologist G. E. Müller, and a teacher of the phenomenologist Stumpf and the act psychologist Brentano. Herbart's successor at Göttingen, Lotze published his influential *Medical Psychology* in 1852. Lotze was a mystic, philosopher, and poet; he is best known in the history of psychology for his theory of local signs, an explanation of space perception which is partly nativistic and partly empiristic. Following Kant, he held that one cannot perceive the world without construing it in spatial terms. The details of the spatial relations among various parts of the retina, between different parts of the skin when touched, and so forth, however, are based upon learning. Long experience with the sensory consequences of certain movements eventually produces a "local sign" for each part of the sensory surface, so that we become aware not only of the fact that we are touched, but also of precisely where we are touched, and learn about the relative locations of various parts of the sensory surface. In his book, which can be considered the first genuine physiological psychology, Lotze also described facial expressions of various emotions, and patterns of expressive movement, a few years before Darwin's well-known work in the same area.

## HELMHOLTZ

An intellectual giant in nineteenth-century science, Hermann von Helmholtz (1821–1894) was a physicist, physiologist, and psychologist; each of these disciplines claims him for its own. His father was an instructor in a military college which had a surgical department, where Helmholtz was trained (on what was then equivalent to the post-World War II American GI bill) as an Army surgeon. He never undertook formal training at a university, but was close to various leading university men of the day, including especially the physiologist Johannes Müller at the University of Berlin. He moved from appointments at Königsberg (where he remained for seven years and where Kant and Herbart had preceded him), then at Bonn (for two years), then at Heidelberg (where he stayed for thirteen highly productive years, and where the young Wundt assisted him in his physiological laboratory), to the University of Berlin, where he spent the last 23 years of his life.

### Physical and Physiological Contributions

In 1847 Helmholtz published a highly significant monograph on the conservation of energy; that the concept was in the Zeitgeist is demonstrated by the fact that it was proposed independently by Mayer, a physician, who published a popular paper on it in the same year. In 1856 there appeared the first volume of Helmholtz's *Handbook of Physiological Optics* (Volumes Two and Three were published in 1860 and 1866); Boring in 1949 still called the work a "gospel in this field." The year 1863 saw the publication of his work on hearing, *Die Tonempfindungen* (*The Sensations of Tone*) which, like his *Optics,* was destined to remain very important in physics, physiology, and psychology. In 1878 there appeared *Die Thatsachen in der Wahrnehmung* (*The Facts of Perception*), a theoretical analysis of perception which elaborated on his influential concept of unconscious inference. Helmholtz accepted an invitation to visit the Chicago World's Fair in 1893; he also visited William James while he was in America (James, incidentally, found him a bore). On the way home he fell down a hatch on his steamer, broke his hip, and never fully recovered; he died in 1894.

Helmholtz made an astonishing number of contributions to the science of his day. Aside from his works in physics, among the most important was his measurement of the speed of the nervous impulse[2] in 1850 at Königsberg, which we described briefly in Chapter 3, and which defied his teacher, Johannes Müller, who had thought that the speed of nervous conduction might be in excess of the speed of light and could probably never be measured. In vision, there were his detailed experiments on color mixture, and the Young-Helmholtz color theory. He also invented the ophthalmoscope, and in his *Handbook* presented a detailed physiological description of the mechanism of accommodation, showing how lens curvature varies with

[2] Helmholtz's father, upon hearing of the experiment and the surprisingly slow measured speed, wrote: "Dear Son, I would as soon believe your result as that we see the light of a star that burned out a million years ago"—inadvertently a singularly apt analogy.

the activity of the ciliary muscle. In hearing, he contributed extensive studies of musical consonance and dissonance, and a specific fiber energies theory of pitch perception, the resonance place theory. The theory, which we met briefly in Chapter 3, held that the basilar membrane in the inner ear is composed of minute fibers of varying length under various degrees of tension, each of which resonates to a different impact frequency.

### Perception and Unconscious Inference

As for general perceptual theory, Helmholtz distinguished between sensation and perception in a manner similar to that later espoused by Titchener, and later still by the mid-twentieth-century transactionalists: sensation is awareness of stimulation, whereas perception is compounded of sensation plus experience. What one receives is the bare sensory pattern, the stimulation of the end organ. Perception is a far more complex cognitive process, involving unconscious inferences based upon past experience: the perception of a chair, for example, involves the addition of a great deal of further material to the bare sensory input, by a process of unconscious inference (*unbewusster Schluss*). Superimposed on the raw input to the receptor surface—that is, on the various wavelengths of light impinging on various parts of the retina—is one's past experience with chairs: that they typically have four legs, are usually made of wood, that they are made to sit on, and so forth. The sensory experience has no meaning as such; perceiving that it is a chair depends upon a complex cognitive judgment, inference, or conclusion, which occurs without the perceiver's awareness. This empiristic view of perception is epitomized by Helmholtz's favorite example: the perception of depth arises by unconscious inference from retinal disparity; that is, the discrepancy between the immediate sensory patterns on the two retinas leads to the unconscious inference of, and hence the perception of, depth. Although unconscious inference is an *unconscious* logical contribution of the perceiver to his percept, Helmholtz argued that the inference is nevertheless irresistible.

Helmholtz also pointed to a derivative principle that is important to the philosophy of science. Because the observer inevitably contributes to his perceptions, Helmholtz argued, any observation, however much it may be supported by information precisely obtained with scientific instruments, inevitably remains a personal observation. It can therefore be affected by the observer's prejudices, past experiences, and personality—an idea that was to be central to the "new look in perception" and the theory of the transactionalists of the middle of the twentieth century.

We should not leave Helmholtz without once again referring to his militant acceptance of scientific materialism in his blood oath, jointly with

DuBois-Reymond, Ludwig, and Brücke, which was mentioned in the preceding chapter under the section "German Materialism."

## FECHNER

Gustav Theodor Fechner (1801–1887), one of the contenders for the title of the first genuine experimental psychologist, was the son of a village pastor. He led a quiet life, obtaining his M.D. and then teaching as a physicist at the University of Leipzig, where for a long time he stayed at the beginning postdoctoral academic teaching level, equivalent to what in the American system would be an assistant professor. He worked many hours doing translations in order to supplement his meager income, and reportedly ruined his eyes; fairly early in his life he retired with a small pension. Some of his research while he taught physics culminated in a significant paper on the theory of the production of electricity by batteries. Although officially a physicist, he was more of a philosopher and a mystic, fighting the materialism of his day in the interests of spiritualism.

### Fechner's Mysticism

Fechner's mysticism was evident in a number of antimaterialistic books that elaborated upon a panpsychic view of man and the world; that is, the view that mind pervades the entire world of nature. These books, many of them tongue in cheek, were published under the pseudonymn of Dr. Mises. One of them made fun of materialism (particularly in the form espoused by Buffon); in it Fechner used the then current methods of rational physiology to go into great detail on the comparative anatomy of angels. In another he tried to prove scientifically by the same methods that the moon is made of green cheese. In response to DuBois-Reymond's materialistic oath, he published another book, which he meant seriously: *Nanna, or Concerning the Mental Life of Plants;* also serious was his *Zend-Avesta, or Concerning Matters of Heaven and the Hereafter.* Interesting as these panpsychic works are, and crucial as they seemed to Fechner in his own thinking, his most influential works for the development of psychology proper were the epoch-making *Elements of Psychophysics* (1860) and also, to a lesser extent, his *Introduction to Aesthetics* (1876); the second of these volumes marks the founding of quantitative, empirical aesthetics.

### Fechner's Law

Fechner's mathematical ability, his predilection for experimentation, and his philosophical beliefs combined to produce psychophysics. Like Spinoza, he held a double aspect view of the mind-body relation, but he went further than Spinoza in that he sought to prove it by writing an equation demonstrating the fundamental identity of the two. He began with the statement of what he called Weber's Law:

$$\frac{\Delta R}{R} = k$$

where $R$ stands for Reiz, or stimulus. Any *jnd,* or just noticeable difference, can be considered a $\Delta R$; *jnd* $= \Delta R$. However, for *jnd,* one can write $\Delta S$ ($S$ for sensation—a just noticeable difference or $\Delta S$ is the minimal physical change in the stimulus required for a minimal change in the sensation), so that the two aspects of matter can be related. This yielded the "fundamental formula":

$$\Delta S = C \left( \frac{\Delta R}{R} \right)$$

Here $S$ is sensation; $R$ is Reiz, or stimulus; and the constant $C$ varies from one sensory modality to another. The left half of the equation is the mental aspect and the right half the physical aspect of the "fundamental substance." Integrating the fundamental formula yields the well-known "measurement formula":

$$S = k \log R$$

that is, the mental sensation is a log function of the stimulus (if the stimulus is measured in terms of increment above threshold); as the stimulus increases linearly, the sensation increases as the logarithm of the stimulus. This equation, incidentally, is largely responsible for the various log measures of physical intensity used today, such as the decibel.

### Psychophysics

Although Fechner's law is still of considerable interest now, especially as exemplified in new versions by Harry Helson and by S. S. Stevens in the 1950s, still more significant was his methodological contribution. In attempting to establish the empirical validity of his law, Fechner did extensive experimental work and invented the psychophysical methods, which now form the basis of measurement in a wide variety of fields, including not only sensation but also psychological testing, the measurement of social attitudes, and many other subfields of psychology.

Fechner used three primary methods; all involve a standard stimulus and a variable stimulus, the latter to be compared with the former: (1) The method of limits—sometimes also called the method of just noticeable differences—involves the serial presentation of successively different values of the variable stimulus, in order, in one's attempt to find the limits of what stimulus values are considered equal to the standard; or, one can begin outside the "equal" region, and slowly change the variable stimulus until it is considered equal to the standard. In this way, one can find the limits of the "equal" zone. (2) The method of constant stimuli, also known as  the method of right and wrong cases, is the most exact of the methods. The subject is presented with pairs composed of the variable stimulus paired in random order with the standard. The subject's task is to judge whether the variable is greater or less than the standard (a variation also permits a judgment of "equal"). (3) The method of reproduction, also called the method of adjustment, or the method of average error, requires the subject to set the variable stimulus so that it appears equal to (or just  greater than or just less than) the standard. These three methods, for the first time, made it possible to measure psychological quantities precisely.[3]

### Experimental Esthetics

For Fechner, psychophysics was really an avocation; his main interest was philosophical. Yet his philosophical works are now largely forgotten, and his main claim to an illustrious place in history lies in the development of psychophysics. But he is also remembered for his attempt to make esthetics experimental in his 1876 book, which contains the formulation and empirical examination of such questions as what are the most pleasing proportions of doors, of animals, and so on, and marks the beginning of an attempt to develop esthetics as a quantitative discipline.

---

[3] As indicated earlier in the paragraph, these methods are applicable not only in the psychophysics laboratory (although, it should be noted, they are, paradoxically, not really appropriate for testing Fechner's law), but also in testing, in the measurement of attitudes, and in industry; for example, a major producer of alcoholic spirits is reported to have developed a sophisticated psychophysical scale of whisky quality.

# 6

# Wilhelm Wundt

Wilhelm Wundt (1832–1920) was the pivotal figure of the era in which experimental psychology became established as a recognized, separate discipline on the intellectual scene. A humorless, aggressive man and an untiring worker, Herr Professor Wundt personified the spirit of post-Fechnerian dry, systematic German psychology.

## THE MAN AND HIS WORKS

Wundt's was a long, productive life, spanning a period of rapid change. In 1832, the year of his birth, the first railroad tracks were laid in Germany, between Nürnberg and Fürth; this was also the year of Goethe's death. People used horses for travel, and used candles to light their homes. Wundt lived until 1920, two years after the end of World War I, by which time electricity, the radio, and the airplane had become commonplace.

Wilhelm Wundt had a very quiet childhood; like Fechner and Nietzsche, he spent his early years in a village pastor's house. Several of his siblings died, and one brother left home early; much of the time he was the only child in the home, but his parents apparently did not pay much attention to him. He was taught by a tutor, a vicar who was his father's assistant. The vicar left after a few years; what home must have meant to Wundt is shown by the fact that Wundt left with him.

When Wundt finally entered school, he did rather poorly, mostly, it seems, because of problems with social adjustment. His mind wandered; his work was so poor that he had to repeat one year, although later he did do well enough to keep up. When he was 19, a relatively early age, he began attending Tübingen University in southern Germany, and thereafter went to Heidelberg, where he studied medicine, and became interested in physiology. His reason for going into medicine was a strictly practical, economic one—he chose it, like some realistic students of today, because he wanted to make a decent living. As several historians have observed, the history of his schooling, and his later works, reveal that Wundt was not really brilliant. He was, however, very hard working, and made full use of what capacity he did have. Perhaps his career demonstrates what strong motivation and an excellent memory, coupled with an adequate, but probably not exceptional, intellect can accomplish.

After a year's internship at Heidelberg, he decided to stop working with patients; apparently he just got tired of them. At this point he went for a year to the University of Berlin to study with Johannes Müller. He received his degree at age 24 and started teaching on his own at Heidelberg. Later he became the equivalent of an instructor there, with the help of Helmholtz, who gave him an assistantship in his laboratory. Wundt directed the exercises in Helmholtz's laboratory course in physiology. He started publishing heavily while at Heidelberg, and continued to be phenomenally prolific throughout the remainder of his career.

It was in 1874 that he obtained his first regular teaching position, at Zürich, Switzerland, as professor of philosophy in inductive logic. In 1875, to Wundt's surprise, he received a call from the University of Leipzig, to become professor of philosophy there; this was a major chair at the time. According to his autobiography, Wundt never knew why the offer came; it might have been because of the 1874 publication of his *Physiological Psychology,* or it may have been largely through Fechner's influence, or perhaps because the physicist Zöllner (who has a well-known perceptual illusion named after him) was impressed with him. At any rate, Wundt became professor of philosophy at Leipzig and stayed there until the end of his life (even though an attempt was made later to get him to go to Berlin, a university with even greater prestige). In 1875 he requested space for demonstrations, and by 1879 he had a genuine psychological research laboratory, the Psychologische Institut, which began as a single room.

At Leipzig he led the quiet life of a scholar; he never was much excited about anything other than his work. Even his wife and family receive no more than one paragraph in his entire autobiography (one might wish to remark drily that this shows how very dedicated he was to his work). His dedication went so far that he analyzed his psychological experiences when he was very seriously ill and near death; at one point in his life he was rather intrigued with the idea of experiencing the process of dying.

During the first few years he had no assistant at the Institut; then, according to Wundt's autobiography, James McKeen Cattell, his student, came to him and said "in typical American fashion," "Herr Professor, you need an assistant, and I shall be he." Cattell served for a time without pay; later the University provided funds for an assistant for Wundt and the Institut grew rapidly.

Many of the books Wundt wrote turned out to be important. In his late twenties, he published two books: one on the theory of muscular movement, and one entitled *Contributions to the Theory of Sense Perception.* In his early thirties, because he needed it for his medical students while teaching for Helmholtz, he published his *Textbook of Human Physiology;* for the same reason, he published another, the *Handbook of Medical Physics.* In 1863 there appeared what might be considered the first comparative psychology: *Lectures on the Minds of Men and Animals.* In 1874 he published his influential and lengthy *Grundzüge der Physiologischen Psychologie (Fundamentals of Physiological Psychology).* In 1881, largely to serve as a publication outlet for research conducted in his laboratory, he started a new psychological journal, *Philosophische Studien,* whose title was later changed to *Psychologische Studien.* During a period of about twelve years he published a series of books on philosophy, each a huge compendious volume: a logic, an ethics, and a major systematic philosophy. His *Outline of Psychology,* which was to undergo many revisions before he died, first appeared in 1896. Between 1900 (when he was 68) and 1920 (when he died at the age of 88) he published a long series of weighty volumes titled *Völkerpsychologie,* a kind of social psychology based on artifacts and institutional products: the volumes dealt with the psychology of language, of art, of law, of religion, and of ethics. Many of these, as well as most of his other books, underwent several revisions before Wundt's death. As several historians have remarked, it is fitting to Wundt's systematic nature that his autobiography appeared in 1920, the year of his death. It has also been proposed that Wundt's later prolific productivity was in large part due to a gift from his assistant Cattell, who gave him an American typewriter—the same typewriter that Cattell had used for his Ph.D. thesis in 1886.

## WUNDT'S SYSTEM

Wundt's approach to psychology was rigidly systematic and logical. He had a place for everything, he classified phenomena and methods into clear-cut categories, and he formulated principles about how the various classes are related.

### The Field of Psychology, Its Methods and Its Task

Wundt preferred to disregard the older definitions of psychology, such as the science of the mind or of the soul, as too metaphysical. He suggested that psychology be defined as the science of consciousness. The subject matter of psychology is *immediate* experience, that is, experience as it is directly, phenomenally, given to the observer, whereas the subject matter of physics and the other natural sciences is *mediate* experience; that is, experience that has been subject to inferences and conceptualizations. Experience is not fixed or static, but rather involves connected events or processes, not objects; experience may *refer* to objects, but is itself a series of subjective processes. Since psychology is the science of consciousness, it is complementary to all of the other sciences, for it studies the immediate experience—that is, psychology studies experience with the subjective left in, whereas the other sciences study experience with subjective factors removed. Psychology was for Wundt basic to, and a prerequisite for, all the cultural disciplines such as philosophy, history, law, and sociology, and preparatory to the philosophical fields of epistemology and ethics.

The methods of psychology are experimentation, and observation without experimentation—still our two major methods. However, his version of experimentation differed from that of later views in that he held that all experimentation in psychology involves introspection, by which he meant the systematic analysis of conscious contents into their elements. Only observation, argued Wundt, can deal with the "higher mental processes," with social phenomena, personality, and the like; these must be studied by way of the cultural products or artifacts of social life: language, art, religion, cultural mores, and ethics. Experimental method, then, is appropriate for the investigation of basic processes such as sensation and association; but observation must be used for the higher mental processes, which are inaccessible to experimentation. It was this conviction that led Wundt to his monumental *Völkerpsychologie,* dealing with the highest problems of psychology. *Völkerpsychologie,* for Wundt, was the keystone of psychology's arch. (One might speculate that Wundt's strong interest in Völkerpsychologie could well have been due to the general romantic tradition in Germany late in the nineteenth century.)

The task of psychology is the analysis of conscious compounds and complexes into their constituent elements, the study of how these compounds are synthesized out of their elements, and the establishment of principles and laws of psychological events. In Wundt's system, the elements together form compounds; compounds together form combinations and complexes. The elements are axiomatically basic. (Many later critics, among them the Gestaltists, raised here the question of whether this may not be putting the cart before the horse. If immediate experience gives us compounds, why not start with these, and derive the elements from the compounds, rather than assume certain elements and then conceptually build up the compounds from them?)

### The Elements of Experience

According to Wundt, all elements are the products of careful analysis and abstraction. The elements can be classified into sensations (referring to the objective contents of experience) and feelings (referring to the subjective contents of experience). Sensations can be classified according to the modality in which they are received; furthermore, they have quality and intensity. Feelings accompany the sensations and their compounds.

Wundt had different classificatory schemes for feelings at various times; perhaps the most influential was his "three-dimensional theory," which used the dimensions of pleasant-unpleasant, tense-relaxed, and excited-calm. This theory was subject to extensive criticism later; it was one of the few instances in which Wundt's pupil, Titchener, differed with his master. Is calm the opposite of excited, as pleasant is the opposite of unpleasant? Or is it rather just the absence of excitement? Furthermore, is there a neutral point between tense and relaxed, or between excited and calm, as there seems to be between pleasant and unpleasant? In addition, Wundt's theory assumed that the three dimensions are independent; but their independence soon came to be questioned on the basis of introspective evidence. The feelings were considered to be associated with certain physiological events, like a raised heartbeat and shallower breathing; Wundt's student Alfred Lehmann tried to establish that each feeling had its own particular physiological correlate, a different pattern for each feeling, but he, like later workers, was unsuccessful in his attempt.

The characteristics of compounds are not, said Wundt, necessarily derivable from the characteristics of the elements—a conception that Wundt took from John Stuart Mill's mental chemistry. The mind performs a creative synthesis on the elements (we shall touch on this idea again presently). The sensations combine into perceptions like tone and space, and the feelings combine into the emotions and other things like the feeling for rhythm, feelings accompanying volition, and so forth. Thus the components of a piano tone, while they never occur separately when that tone on the piano is struck, can be made to occur separately, as with appropriately driven tuning forks.

### Consciousness and Attention

Consciousness is a combination of compounds, by Wundt's definition; the basis of consciousness is the structure of the animal organism. (The brain, which conditions consciousness, has separate organs for language, for writing, and so forth—a conception reminiscent of faculty psychology and phrenology.)

One of the major processes of consciousness is attention, which makes certain parts of the conscious field clearer than the background. The product of attention is a condition of very clear perception—the area attended to is the clearest part of consciousness. Apperception is the process of bringing things to attention, that is, to clearest perception; here the word "apperception" is used as it was by Leibnitz, not by Herbart—that is, as clear, complex perception, not as a global attribute of consciousness and its receptivity to new ideas. Wundt distinguished between the *focus* and the *field* of consciousness; attention involves bringing things into the focus; those things that are not in the focus are in the field. This conception is in some respects similar to Edgar Rubin's later distinction between figure and ground, which the gestalt psychologists were to make a major part of their theoretical system.

### Association

How are elements combined into compounds, and simple compounds combined into still higher-order complexes? The process is one of association, which occurs in three different forms—fusion, assimilation, and complication: (1) Fusion is a combination of elements that never occur separately, as, for example, a piano tone; one does not hear separately the pure-tone elements that compose it. (2) Assimilation is the fusion of elements, not all of which are present in consciousness; for example, when one is reading a word, one may not be aware of the particular letters, or of the particular type face. Assimilation involves supplementing what is perceived by elements that are not in consciousness—a conception that has something in common with Hamilton's redintegration. Finally, (3) a complication is a compound of elements from different sense modalities, as in flavor (which is composed of taste, smell, temperature sense, and possibly tactual, kinesthetic, and visual components).

### Mental Development

Whereas association was divided into three categories, the psychology of mental development was separated into two. There is the study of child development, that is, the study of the development of psychological processes in the individual; then there is the problem of the cultural development of groups, which involves the study of language, law, art, religion, and so forth. The two were seen as entirely distinct fields.

### Psychic Causality and Creative Synthesis

Wundt's answer to the mind-body problem was a psychophysical parallelism: the same causal laws operate in the mental as in the physical sphere. What he meant by causality, however, was similar to Hume's analysis. All that he referred to was regularity and lawfulness—the principle of psychic causality holds that mental events are just as orderly as physical ones. Wundt held that experience is unitary, even though one can conceptually divide it into mediate (the physical sciences) and immediate (psychology). The two kinds of experience are mutually consistent. Since mediate experience involves causality, causality is inherent in all experience and thus also in immediate experience; mental causality cannot possibly contradict physical causality.

Although mental contents are compounded of elements, mental activity culminates in a creative synthesis. The mind acts on the mental elements, producing creative, unifying combinations; the result of the creative synthesis is different from the sum of the elements making it up. Here Wundt anticipated some central ideas in later gestalt theory.

## WUNDT'S LABORATORY AND STUDENTS

Wundt's laboratory flourished for many years. About one-half of the work performed there was on sensation and perception, most of it with a strong physiological flavor. There was also much research on reaction time; Lange's finding that muscular reaction time is shorter than sensorial came to be hailed as one of the more significant discoveries in this work. Attention, association, and feeling, as for example the investigations of Lehmann referred to earlier, complete the list of areas studied.[1]

Much of the work emanating from Wundt's laboratory, including his own voluminous writings, involved Wundt in controversies. It seems he easily became irritated and lost his temper in these controversies, usually being the one who made the first personal attacks. (Wundt's name, incidentally, is an old spelling of a German word meaning "sore, wounded, chafed or galled.") One might guess that his vituperation was perhaps another reflection of the social ineptitude that led to trouble during his school years.

Before long, students flocked to Wundt to learn about the new psychology. Leipzig became the world center for psychology, with a very active laboratory, and with the first truly systematic experimental psychologist, in the person of Wundt. He and his students raised the important issues one after another, and were doing something about them. Furthermore, Wundt's approach epitomized the Zeitgeist; it exhibited the influence of all of the eight trends mentioned in Part I. The work was physiological and biological, with quantification a major aim. It was performed in a highly active research

---

[1] Although Wundt's work has sometimes been criticized as suffering from a certain narrowness, this criticism may be somewhat inappropriate. After all, this was just the bare beginning of genuine experimental psychology. Wundt can hardly be blamed that there were no studies of learning in the early years of his laboratory; that kind of work was not yet in the Zeitgeist and had to wait until after 1885, when Ebbinghaus' monograph on memory was published.

laboratory, with a strictly elementistic, atomistic orientation; the goal was to reduce all of consciousness to its elements. The theory behind the research, and much of the research itself, was associationistic, and scientific materialism was evident in the effort to relate psychological to physiological events. Finally, the emphasis on empirical, experimental methods, as well as the idea that mental life is the product of the compounding of experience, and that most mental events depend upon past experience, exemplified the critical empiricist, and empirist tradition.

Many of the students who came to Wundt were to be important in Europe and in the United States in later years. Among these were Emil Kraepelin, the psychiatrist who was to be responsible for the classification of mental disorders which, in modified form, is still in use during the latter part of the twentieth century. Hugo Münsterberg was brought to Harvard by William James in order to enlighten the uninformed American natives about the exciting new developments in Germany and to carry on experimental research in psychology. Alfred Lehmann began the tradition of trying to find physiological correlates of emotion, and Carl Lange provided the first formulation of what was later to be the renowned James-Lange theory of emotion. Then there was Oswald Külpe, who was to found his own highly influential rival school at the University of Würzburg.

Among Wundt's American students were G. Stanley Hall, later at Clark University, who wrote on child psychology, adolescence, and senescence, among other areas. James McKeen Cattell, Wundt's first assistant, and later a major figure at Columbia, was to start the long and active tradition of testing people—especially college students—for individual differences. E. B. Titchener, later at Cornell University, became the center of United States structuralism, a school against which others could contrast their views during the first quarter of the twentieth century. H. C. Warren produced the first dictionary of psychology. G. M. Stratton, later at California, undertook classical studies of vision with inverting lenses. C. H. Judd, first a professor of education and then later Dean of the School of Education at Chicago, wrote a major psychology of social institutions, to some extent patterned on Wundt's *Völkerpsychologie*.

Wundt, then, was the new experimental psychology personified. Although he has gradually slipped into the stream of history—in that relatively little work is now going on which is still directly influenced by his formulations and experiments—a remarkable portion of modern psychology was given a major impetus by Wundt's work. He and his students helped to define and to start work on many of the questions of interest to the psychologist of the second half of the twentieth century.

# 7

# The Contemporary
# Scene in the Age
# of Wundt

Significant though he was in the history of psychology, Wundt was, of course, not the only important psychologist at the end of the nineteenth century. Three of Wundt's contemporaries were making their own independent way, and attracting students, although they did not have quite the influence Wundt had in that time: Franz Brentano, Carl Stumpf, and G. E. Müller. Two nonpsychologists of the day also had a profound impact upon later psychology: the physiologist Ewald Hering and the physicist Ernst Mach. Wundt's student Oswald Külpe has already been mentioned; and then there was the quiet and independent Hermann Ebbinghaus, who has also been briefly referred to. In England, the versatile Sir Francis Galton was helping to lay the foundations of the psychology of individual differences. Things were also beginning to stir in the United States, but we shall leave consideration of the American developments for the next chapter.

## THREE CONTEMPORARY PSYCHOLOGISTS

### Brentano

Franz Brentano (1838–1917) founded the act school of psychology, whose tenets included ideas fundamental in later schools as diverse as functionalism, gestalt psychology, and behaviorism. He came from a celebrated family, originally merchants in Italy, who settled near Bonn on the Rhine River. The Brentano clan included Clemens Brentano, a lyrical poet who collected folk songs (the world-renowned composer Gustav Mahler used this material in his musical work), Clemens' sister Bettina, who was one of Goethe's paramours, Heinrich Brentano, who during the 1950s was Foreign Minister of Germany, and there is also the branch of the family who owns the huge Brentano's bookstore in New York City.

Franz Brentano's life was full of crises. A restless man and independent thinker, he studied for the priesthood; he earned his Ph.D. in philosophy at Tübingen and was ordained the same year, 1864. His career as a Catholic priest ran into difficulty because of his liberal views (opposition to the doctrine of the infallibility of the Pope), which eventually led him to leave the Church. Later, he had an intense, long love affair, and finally married his beloved; not many years later she died, leaving him heartbroken. He traveled a great deal in Switzerland and Italy, and taught at several universities in Germany and Austria, including Würzburg and Vienna. A man of strong convictions, he was a pacifist, and was plagued during the last two decades of his life by progressive blindness, which, to his exasperation, interfered with his struggles to write philosophy.

It was in 1874, the year in which Wundt's *Physiological Psychology* appeared, that Brentano published his most important psychological work, *Psychology from the Empirical Point of View*—which presented views that were strikingly different from those of Wundt. Brentano held that it was a mistake to make psychology predominantly or exclusively physiological. Although he agreed that psychology should be empirical, Brentano felt it should not necessarily be experimental—if by experiment one means tedious systematic variation of an independent variable and concomitant measurement of a dependent variable.

Experiments are basically of two kinds: crucial and systematic. Crucial experiments serve to decide between two opposite conceptions, but, Brentano advised, one should not engage in unproductive systematic experiments, which tend to be pedestrian, and only yield a somewhat more precise description of experience—not a very useful function in the early stages of the development of psychology. One should try to systematize psychology, and, when there are doubts, perform an "experimentum crucis." Crucial experiments help decide about important issues, but systematic experiments do not. Brentano further declared that systematic experiments may produce an overemphasis on method and create a blindness to the main issues facing psychology. This clearly is a very different position from that of Wundt, who championed thorough systematic experimentation. (It can be argued that the distinction has a flavor that is too definite, too final; it is not always easy to tell whether an experiment is systematic or crucial. Furthermore, blindness to important substantive issues may not be a characteristic of a method, but rather of a poor experimenter. Also, it is by no means always possible to perform a crucial experiment—examples abound in mid-twentieth-century psychology, as in transposition, latent learning, the continuity-noncontinuity issue, in which experiments first thought to be crucial turned out not to be decisive after all. Brentano was perhaps less of an experimenter than a theoretician.)

Another major difference between Brentano and Wundt lay in the distinction between psychology and physics. For Brentano, physical phenomena are self-contained, and do not refer to other objects; they have an *intrinsic completeness.* Mental phenomena, on the other hand, have *immanent objectivity.* That is, they refer to content, *imply* an object or a referent. All mental phenomena are acts referring to outside objects; objects are immanent in mental acts. The mental acts include ideating, recalling, perceiving, sensing, judging, loving and hating, feeling, wishing, intending to do something, and so forth. It is because mental events are all oriented "outside," because all acts imply objects, refer to something else, that Brentano's approach has been called "act psychology," as contrasted with the more static mental content orientation of the kind that characterized much of Wundt's work.

Brentano did not have a very large number of students, but he had a wide influence nevertheless. Külpe, trained primarily by Wundt, was later an admirer and follower of Brentano, and perhaps his most outstanding one; although the British psychologists Ward, Stout, and McDougall did not study with Brentano, they were all influenced by him—the British psychology of the late nineteenth and the early twentieth century had a distinct Brentano flavor. McDougall, for that matter, translated the German word "Akt" into the English word "behavior," defining psychology as the study of behavior—almost a decade before John Watson did. It may also be of interest to note that Sigmund Freud attended Brentano's lectures for a year.

### Stumpf

Carl Stumpf (1848–1936), who also studied for a year with Brentano, was an outstanding figure of the time. Devoted to music, he is reported to have played some six different instruments very competently. Stumpf occupied the chair at Berlin for 26 years, after which it passed to the gestalt psychologist Köhler. Stumpf founded the Berlin Psychological Laboratory, which concentrated under his guidance primarily on work in space perception and in audition; in 1883 he published an influential *Tonpsychologie,* a major supplement to, and rival of, Helmholtz's work on tonal sensation.

Stumpf held that the primary data are "phenomena"; this led to the philosophy and methodology of phenomenology. Stumpf maintained that phenomenology, the unbiased examination of experience as it comes, is preliminary to all sciences, both psychology and the physical sciences. Psychology studies mental functions (much like Brentano's acts), and relations among phenomena. It is inadvisable to decide a priori on appropriate elements as Wundt had tried to do. One of Stumpf's students, Edmund Husserl, developed the later highly influential philosophy of phenomenology in voluminous, abstruse, and difficult-to-read writings.

Also, all three of the earliest gestalt psychologists—Köhler, Koffka, and Wertheimer—who were to make extensive use of the phenomenological method, studied at one time or another with Stumpf. Stumpf's philosophical position had a lasting effect on psychology, and especially philosophy, and his work in hearing and in the phenomenological method has remained influential for many years.

## G. E. Müller and His Students

Georg Elias Müller (1850–1934) was the experimenter of the trio of Müller, Brentano, and Stumpf. Whereas others generally had their students conduct the experiments, Müller did them himself. He held the Göttingen chair for 40 years; this chair had been held before by Lotze for 37 years, and before that for 8 years by Herbart.

After his Ph.D. on attention, Müller continued to do extensive work in a wide variety of areas: psychophysics, vision, physiological psychology, and also memory, after Ebbinghaus's fundamental work. Müller was somewhat disturbed by phenomenology and gestalt psychology when they came on the scene, and after his retirement wrote a polemical critique, published in 1923, in which he maintained that not only was this all known before, but that several of his students had done much of the work that was later considered fundamental to gestalt psychology.

There can be no question that Müller's students did make major contributions, many of them to be taken up by the gestalt school. Thus Harry Helson compiled a history of gestalt psychology for his doctorate; this history was published in several installments in the *American Journal of Psychology*. And then there was Adolph Jost, well-known for his work in memory; under Müller, Jost studied the effects of distributed and massed practice, and had a law named after him—that old associations profit more from a single repetition than do equally strong newer ones. David Katz, Müller's assistant for 11 years, and later professor of psychology at the University of Stockholm, published a detailed phenomenology of color vision. Narziss Ach developed the concept of determining tendency, or set, so important in the research of the Würzburg school and adopted and modified in the 1930s by Kurt Lewin. E. R. Jaensch worked on eidetic imagery and later on personality types and traits; and Edgar Rubin, later professor of psychology at the University of Copenhagen, obtained his Ph.D. with Müller for fundamental work on the distinction between figure and ground. There were many other students as well, and a wide variety of areas was studied in Müller's laboratory. Müller is perhaps best remembered as the indefatigable and dedicated early experimenter in the new psychology.[1]

---

[1] Müller was, though, reported to be not very gracious to persons who visited Göttingen and wanted to see the laboratory. This was said to be because he felt that the equipment at Göttingen was quite meager compared with that at Leipzig.

## TWO NONPSYCHOLOGISTS AT PRAGUE

### Hering

Ewald Hering (1834–1918) was a physiologist, succeeding J. E. Purkinje at the University of Prague, in Czechoslovakia. Purkinje, also a physiologist, had used a phenomenological approach, and had, among other things, discovered brightness shifts with dark adaptation. Hering too was a phenomenologist and was interested in vision. He was also concerned with space perception, about which he held a nativistic position.

Hering proposed a new color theory based upon the phenomena of negative afterimages. There are three kinds of cones in the retina, he argued, the red-green, the yellow-blue, and the black-white. The cold colors—green, blue, and black—produce an assimilation, a building up, or anabolism; the warm colors—red, yellow, and white—result in dissimilation, breaking down, or catabolism, of the substance in the retinal cones. This theory was soon severely criticized, because it seemed to go against the all-or-none law—how could the same fiber send one message for anabolism, and a different one for catabolism? But the theory again became very influential in the middle of the twentieth century, when it was discovered that such an opponent-process mechanism can, and does, exist: R. DeValois found that one process may reduce, the other increase, the rate of neural firing engaged in spontaneously during the resting stage.

In 1870 Hering published a monograph on memory, in which he argued that in a sense inorganic matter can demonstrate memory. A folded piece of paper, a hammered nail that had been bent and had been straightened, will subsequently fold or bend more readily in the same place. William James was to use this conception in his writing some twenty years later.

Hering was also a fine experimenter and gadgeteer. Among other things, he invented a stereoscope and the Hering papers, a standardized series of greys from white to black, which were still in use over half a century later.

### Mach

Ernst Mach (1838–1916), physicist and mathematician, spent his most important years at Prague. In spite of his professional identification as a physicist, he published much experimental research on vision, space perception, hearing, and the sense of time, as well as a full-length book on the perception of rotation.

Perhaps Mach's most significant work in psychology, though, was his *Analysis of Sensations* (1886). Mach was interested in the fundamental bases of science, and agreed with Wundt that the data of all sciences are sensations or experience. Furthermore, he accepted Kant's notion that space and time are fundamental to all sensory processes. Since the raw material of all sciences is sensation, he argued, all the sciences are basically the same. They differ only in their content; different ones study different classes of sensations. His work was to have a major influence on the phenomenologists and, later, the logical positivists. Among his more frequently cited contributions was a sketch of his room as seen by one eye, about which he commented that this percept was all that he, as physicist, psychologist, human being, was actually given. His attempt to determine the experimental, epistemological bases of all knowledge makes him also, then, an important early figure in what was later to develop into the positivist movement in philosophy.

But Mach is, of course, best known for his contributions in mathematics and physics; his name has been given to the unit of measurement for supersonic speeds: nowadays everybody knows that Mach 4 means four times the speed of sound.

## KÜLPE AND THE WÜRZBURG SCHOOL

### Külpe

Oswald Külpe (1862–1915), a Latvian by birth, had a varied career as student and professor, moving from one university to another, and originally wavering among psychology, philosophy, and history. He studied at Leipzig, then Berlin, then at Göttingen with Müller (with whom he began his doctoral dissertation), then went for a year to the University at Dorpat to study history, and finally returned to Leipzig, where he was to work with Wundt for eight years, becoming his second assistant (succeeding Cattell). After Leipzig he went to Würzburg, where he became the moving spirit of what was to be called the Würzburg school. Külpe was at Würzburg between 1894 and 1909 (it was at Würzburg, incidentally, that Roentgen, in 1896, made his discovery of x-rays). In 1909 Külpe went to Bonn, and thence to Munich; he died at the early age of 53.

He wandered not only from university to university, but also from field to field. Starting with an interest in history, he switched to philosophy, then moved to esthetics, music, and finally psychology; after further wavering, he settled primarily on philosophy and psychology. During his philosophical phase, he wrote five popular books on philosophy for laymen, including one on Kant, and another on philosophers of the turn of the century. While at Leipzig, Külpe met and roomed with Titchener; apparently he was at first "repulsed by Titchener's British brusqueness," but soon overcame his dislike. Titchener regarded Külpe and his work very highly, and in fact translated some of Külpe's writings into English.

Külpe's psychological views moved gradually from the psychology of Wundt (as exemplified by Külpe's early *Outline of Psychology*) towards that of

Brentano; this change contrasts sharply with Titchener's uncompromising Wundtianism. According to his contemporaries, in spite of his early animosity toward Titchener, Külpe was a pleasant, charming person, who got along well with everybody. He was a hard worker, wrote a great deal, and whatever he wrote was thoughtful. He made it a matter of principle to serve as a subject in his students' experiments in order to know what they were doing—but he never made himself a co-author on his students' works.

### The Würzburg School and Its Students

The Würzburg school became an important rival to Leipzig. Much experimental work was performed, a substantial proportion of it producing results inconsistent with a thoroughgoing Wundtian position. (Titchener urged Külpe to write a summary of the work from the Würzburg laboratory, but Külpe never got around to it.) The major problems studied included esthetics—Külpe was an excellent musician—attention, association, and particularly thinking; the Würzburg school is best known in subsequent history for its work on imageless thought. Wundt had said that it is impossible to experiment with the higher mental processes, including thinking; Külpe, the renegade, said "Why not try?" and went ahead and experimented with it. His fresh approach attracted many of the best students of the day; they flocked to him to help him try to find an element of thinking, commensurate with Wundt's elements of sensation and feeling. But Külpe and his students found none; hence they concluded that thinking can be imageless. The Wundtians called this finding negative, but it can surely be considered positive, in that it led to important concepts such as set, which are still with us.

Among the Ph.D. theses written under Külpe was one by Marbe on levels of consciousness, which concerned itself with the difficulty of shifting among levels of thought. Wertheimer, later at the center of the gestalt school, wrote his doctoral dissertation under Külpe on the use of the word association technique in the determination of guilt. Another was undertaken by Watt; it demonstrated the strong influence of set, attitude, or instruction. A subject, given a problem, develops a task set, or an "Einstellung," and thought runs automatically once the task has been accepted—a principle still very important in the middle of the twentieth century, as, for example, in the well-known work of A. S. Luchins on the effect of set on the water-jar problem.

Narziss Ach, after having studied with Müller at Göttingen, came to Würzburg and continued his famous work on the determining tendency: the original set to solve a problem is not enough, but must persist throughout the entire thinking process, during the phase of judging various attempted solutions, and so forth; in uttering a sentence, for example, the first part determines to some extent the characteristics of the remaining words in the sentence. This approach to thinking was similar to that of Brentano: thought and action are identical, thinking is a process, and it is unprofitable simply to examine the static mental content at any given moment. This emphasis on the directionality of thought is also somewhat similar to the gestalt concept of insight, made much of later by the gestalt psychologists Köhler and Wertheimer; it can also be seen as a forerunner of interest in sequential dependencies in behavior, a focus of research among many later quantitative psychologists. The outcome of the Würzburg experiments, then, was not negative, but, rather, began a chain of influential new work.

## EBBINGHAUS

Hermann Ebbinghaus (1850–1909), an inventive, ingenious experimenter, was not directly associated with any particular school. He became the equivalent of an associate professor at Berlin, but when Stumpf was brought in over his head as professor, he left for Breslau. Ebbinghaus wrote an excellent *Outline of Psychology*, whose style has been compared to that of William James's book *Principles of Psychology*, famous for its felicitous writing. Ebbinghaus was also the first to publish a paper on the intelligence testing of school children, using a completion task which is still included in some current test batteries. This work, later taken up by Binet, Simon, and others, was to burgeon into the vast mental testing movement in the United States in the first half of the twentieth century. In 1890 he founded, with Arthur König, a new journal on the psychology and physiology of the sense organs, which broke the monopoly on German psychological journals previously held by Wundt with his *Philosophische Studien*.

Ebbinghaus's most significant contribution, however, was published in 1885: the extremely influential monograph *Über das Gedächtnis (On Memory)*. In the late 1870s, while Ebbinghaus was spending three post-Ph.D. years in England and France, studying philosophy, he picked up a copy of Fechner's *Elements of Psychophysics* at a secondhand bookstall on the Rive Gauche in Paris. He was deeply impressed by the work, and it inspired him to try his hand at a comparably precise and experimental investigation of memory. The result, after years of work, was the monograph, which reported the results of a prodigiously thorough series of replicated experiments which Ebbinghaus had patiently performed on himself; this was the first time that learning and memory were studied experimentally and quantitatively. Since the meaning of material influences how easily it is learned, Ebbinghaus invented *sinnlose Silben*—literally, "meaningless syllables," but nowadays rendered as "nonsense syllables"—constructed of consonant, vowel, then consonant, with meaningful words excluded. His primary techniques were complete mastery and savings. That is, he counted how many trials it took to memorize a list of syllables; alternatively, for the savings method, he memorized some material at a particular time, then had no further contact with it for a while, and finally determined how much easier it was to relearn it later on—the difference in the number of trials required to relearn, relative to the number required for original learning, or the saving, could then constitute a measure of the amount retained.

In addition to the basic memorization experiment, Ebbinghaus undertook many variations: he studied the effect of the time interval between learning and test, varied the amount of material learned, changed the order of the syllables, and so forth. Ebbinghaus's account included a detailed examination of how the curve of retention was influenced by the amount of material; he also studied the strength of forward and backward associations ("remote associations"), as well as the effects of overlearning. Later applications of his method resulted in Jost's and Müller's work on massed compared with distributed practice, in Müller's studies of the influence of intervening material, and ultimately in studies of retroactive inhibition by many people, problem areas still very important in the memory research of the second half of the twentieth century, as in the investigations of B. J. Underwood. Another development was the study of reminiscence, perhaps a somewhat misleading name for the finding that material may be somewhat better remembered a short time after original learning than immediately after it, especially if the original memorization trials were massed.

The spirit and method of Ebbinghaus's work continued to be central to psychology long after his death. This pioneer effort was a manifestation of atomism or elementism, of structuralism, and of course of associationism; perhaps most important, it demonstrated that it is possible actually to experiment quantitatively with learning and memory. This same kind of approach, involving the serial learning of items, was extended in the twentieth century to the study of maze learning by animals, as well as to a wide variety of additional problems in animal and human learning.[2]

## GALTON AND OTHER BRITISH PSYCHOLOGISTS

Developments that were to have a profound influence on twentieth-century psychology were not, of course, limited to Germany or to Continental Europe. The English tradition exemplified by John Stuart Mill, by Charles Darwin, by Herbert Spencer, and by Alexander Bain had perhaps its greatest original genius in the latter half of the nineteenth century in Sir Francis Galton (1822–1911), a versatile, restless and inventive man, the founder of the eugenics movement and a major contributor to the mental testing movement that was to snowball in America in the twentieth century. Other

---

[2] It may also be of interest to the student of the history of psychology to note that it was Ebbinghaus who made the insightful comment that psychology has a long past but only a short history.

British psychologists—Ward, Stout, McDougall—also contributed to the growing new discipline of psychology.

### Galton

Ten years after the publication of Darwin's *The Origin of Species,* Galton came out with a book, *Hereditary Genius,* in which he traced the family trees of outstanding people, and proposed that Darwin's principle holds for the inheritance of particular human psychological traits as well as for various morphological characteristics of other species. The family pedigree method, with the finding that special gifts—and stigmata—tend to run in families, led Galton to suggest that selective breeding of humans (or eugenics) would appear desirable in order to improve the stock of homo sapiens—an idea that generated much heated discussion.

Galton's convictions about the importance of heredity in human behavior and morphology led him to an analysis of human races in terms of their adaptation to their particular ecological circumstances, and also to an abiding interest in individual differences. He studied quantitatively, by questionnaire, the incidence of different kinds of imagery (visual, auditory, olfactory, and so forth) in different people, and also measured "free associations" to standard words experimentally. His quantitative bent led to the invention of the coefficient of correlation, an index of the degree to which two characteristics covary; this work was in the tradition of Laplace, Gauss, and Quetelet, the pioneers in statistics, and was later ably carried on by Karl Pearson at the Galton laboratory in the University of London.

### Ward, Stout, and Sully

James Ward (1843–1925) tried to found a laboratory of experimental psychology at Cambridge, but he turned out to be more of a systematizer than an experimentalist. His system was presented in its most elaborate form in his *Psychological Principles* (1918), although its first statement appeared in an article in the 1886 edition of the *Encyclopaedia Britannica*. Ward's psychology was tripartite; he divided psychological processes into cognition, feeling, and conation. More popular than Ward's writings were the systematic textbooks of George Frederick Stout (1860–1944), who, like Ward, was more of a systematizer than an experimentalist, and also the works of James Sully (1842–1923), another systematic British psychologist who was influential in his day.

### McDougall

William McDougall (1871–1938) was another figure in the evolutionary tradition. He developed his own hormic or purposive psychology, emphasizing particularly the conative or striving part of Ward's division. His evolutionary interest led him to a study of human sentiments and instincts, to the writing of a highly influential early text on social psychology, and eventually to experiments on acquired characteristics. He taught at London and Oxford, then at Harvard and Duke, but even though he was in America for 24 years he has been characterized as remaining British in outlook throughout his entire career. Indeed, although he had been the first to characterize psychology as the science of behavior, he rescinded this definition later because he meant something quite different by the term "behavior" than the ultraobjective American behaviorists did.

### Animal Behaviorists

Another part of psychology growing out of Darwinism was interest in animal behavior. George John Romanes (1848–1894), C. Lloyd Morgan (1852–1936), Jacques Loeb (1859–1924), Leonard T. Hobhouse (1864–1929), and Sir John Lubbock (1834–1913) belong in this tradition. The study of lower animals became more relevant to an understanding of man once the principle of evolution had placed man into the context of other species. Romanes, who knew Darwin personally and well, wrote an early book on comparative psychology, *Animal Intelligence*; it was published in 1882. Morgan wrote several books on animal and comparative psychology, and in 1894 propounded his version of the law of parsimony, which we met in Chapter 4 as Lloyd Morgan's Canon. In Chapter 4 we also mentioned Loeb's work on tropisms, done in Germany; Hobhouse undertook experiments on animal behavior and reported them in his *Mind in Evolution* in 1901; Lubbock presented detailed observations on the complex social behavior of ants and other insects in a work published in 1892.

### THE CHARACTER OF THE "NEW" PSYCHOLOGY

The European psychological Zeitgeist toward the end of the nineteenth century, then, was characterized by what was seen by many people in many places as an exciting new approach to the study of mental phenomena.

It was experimental, evolutionary, primarily introspective, and dealt with experience and consciousness; it was elementaristic and associationistic. The chief emphasis was on the study of conscious content, but there was also some attention to act or function. It resulted from the converging trends and tendencies before 1860, each of which contributed its distinctive stamp to the new formulation. Within the next decades, laboratories had been established at Leipzig, Berlin, Würzburg, and Göttingen, as well as at some lesser places. Physiology was the keystone in the study of sensory phenomena, and Wundt's highly significant work even called itself physiological psychology. The influence of evolution and other biological concepts was particularly strong in British psychology and in Wundt's lectures on the minds of men and animals; it also emerged in the interest in animal behavior, late in the nineteenth century and particularly in the twentieth. The atomistic trend was evident in the concentration on elements, as in Wundt's systematic introspection, in Ebbinghaus's nonsense syllables, and in Külpe's futile search for the element of thought. Quantification was at the core of Fechner's work and that of later psychophysicists, was a major goal in the study of reaction time, and was basic to Ebbinghaus's elegant savings method and Galton's interest in individual differences.

The definition of psychology in terms of experience, the emphasis upon the introspective method, and the attempt to understand the contents of awareness, all exemplified the critical empiricist trend, as did the fact that everybody was busily doing experiments, and trying to explain everything in terms of past experience. Associationism was the rule in approaches to learning, and also to perception; Ebbinghaus, Wundt, Müller, and others were much concerned with the compounding of elements and with serial learning, and Helmholtz and his associationistic doctrine of unconscious inference played a major role in attempts to understand perception. Scientific materialism had been established by Helmholtz, by DuBois-Reymond, and others; concern with the "soul" was no longer really relevant to psychology, and almost everybody was trying to reduce psychological phenomena to physiological ones.

# 8

# William James and American Psychology

Although experimental psychology was born and raised in Europe, particularly in Germany, it emigrated to the United States at the end of the nineteenth century. By the second or third decade of the twentieth century, psychology's center of gravity was definitely in America.

## AMERICAN PSYCHOLOGY BEFORE JAMES

Before William James brought the new European psychology across the Atlantic, American psychology had been philosophical and moralistic. To the extent that there were any American psychologists at all before James, they were mostly church men.

One of the early original thinkers was the Puritan, Jonathan Edwards (1703–1758), a president of Princeton University who lies buried on that campus. Edwards had a stormy career in the Church before he got to Princeton, moving from Congregationalism to Calvinistic Presbyterianism. In 1754 he published a treatise in which he supported, with persuasive argument and logical reasoning, the Calvinistic creed that there is no free will, that everything is predestined, and that it is impossible to escape one's destiny.

Writers who came after Edwards in United States psychology were generally less provocative and original; as was true of most earlier and later authors, they typically repeated the ideas of others. Most of the works were written in an attempt to influence students' morals, to get them to think and act right—perhaps as futile an endeavor then as now. Among such books, purporting to be about psychology, was one by Henry Tappan, President of the University of Michigan; the 1860s saw another by Noah Porter, President of Yale, and in the 1870s one was published by James McCosh, President of Princeton. Somehow university presidents seemed to consider moral psychology their special responsibility. The emphasis on moral issues characteristic of these works exemplified the Puritan Zeitgeist that pervaded the United States in the eighteenth and nineteenth centuries.

## WILLIAM JAMES

### The Man and His Works

William James (1842–1910), brilliant, tolerant, cosmopolitan, has often been called the first true American psychologist. A contemporary of Wundt, James was an entirely different kind of person. He came from a Boston family, led a fairly quiet life, and traveled widely in Europe and elsewhere. His well-known novelist brother Henry James was also a world traveler; Henry finally spent most of his years in England. Although he did so geographically, William never got away from Harvard academically. He received his M.D. degree there, and became particularly interested in physiology; his first teaching appointment at Harvard was as assistant professor of physiology. Later he taught some courses in philosophy and eventually was made professor of philosophy, then a professor of psychology, and finally again professor of philosophy. James suffered from poor health throughout much of his life, but nevertheless managed an output that was both voluminous and qualitatively highly regarded both by his contemporaries and by later critics.

For psychology, his most important contribution was his two-volume *Principles of Psychology* (1890). In 1892 he published a condensed version of the *Principles: Psychology, Briefer Course*, which the graduate students of the first half of the twentieth century affectionately called the "Jimmy," and which may well have been the first genuine best seller in psychology. In the 1890s James also published a smaller volume, *Talks to Teachers on Psychology;* this showed his interest in educational psychology. About the turn of the century came *Varieties of Religious Experience*. Then there were several philosophical works, among them *Pragmatism,* which had a tremendous impact, *A Pluralistic Universe, The Meaning of Truth,* and *Is Life Worth Living?*, written during his last years.

Although James was chiefly a philosopher, he was also very much of a psychologist. Rather than a scientist, he was more a literary man—an excellent writer. He read very widely, and was actively and creatively critical of what he read, but very fair in his criticism. He was "naive" toward facts and theories, in the best sense of being free to look, but was sophisticated and incisive in his interpretations of what he found. Erudite and yet not pedantic, he had many new ideas and could express them in highly colorful prose. He permitted his ideas to lead him wherever they wished, and in this sense he was eclectic; it is not accidental that later behaviorists quoted him favorably, as did the functionalists; gestalt ideas are also to be found in his writings.

### The Principles of Psychology

James's *Principles of Psychology* is essentially a collection of essays. As a whole, it is much less rigidly organized than Wundt's systematic book. Although it is impossible to shuffle Wundt's chapters, one can readily jump about among James's. The chapters seem to follow one another almost haphazardly.

It was James, in his chapter on habit, who came out with the statement that "habit is the enormous flywheel of society," a doctrine that is characteristic of the concentration upon habit and rote learning so prevalent in American psychology and sociology since James. Like many of his intellectual predecessors, James argued for a physiological basis of habit: repeated activity produces a pathway in the brain, through which subsequent energy is channeled. This simple and compelling idea, in various slightly modified forms, was to be *the* physiological theory of learning in psychology for the next three or four decades, notably in the writings of E. L. Thorndike and John B. Watson, until Karl Lashley showed that it was neurological nonsense—and it even persisted after that. Central to the theory is an atomistic notion of concatenated discharges, of reflex paths, the "deepening of ruts," a conception of isolated sensory processes and muscular contractions, or reflex arcs, hooked together. The more modern version is bonds or connections between stimuli and responses. James also originated the idea of response-produced stimuli, a construct central to the later work of Clark Hull and his followers, of E. R. Guthrie, and of Charles Osgood. For James, following Hering, the brain process of memory is a function of the plasticity of organic matter.

In the field of emotion, James is known for the theory which he promulgated independently of the Danish physiologist Carl Lange, who published a similar idea at about the same time. The James-Lange theory is not that we perceive an emotion-arousing situation, become emotional about it, and then suffer bodily changes because of the emotion, but rather that the perception of the situation leads to a bodily state, and the awareness of the bodily state is the emotion. Thus according to the theory the sequence is not that we lose our fortune, are sorry, and weep, or meet a bear, are frightened, and run, but rather that we feel sorry *because* we cry when we lose our fortune, are frightened *because* we run. The chief significance of the theory lay in the fact that many people took issue with it in the next years; it generated a great deal of research and interest.

James's description of the stream of consciousness, another contribution for which he is deservedly remembered, still appeared quite modern more than three-quarters of a century after it was formulated. This stream, James wrote, has five major characteristics. Thought is personal; that is, it is *my* thought. Secondly, it is constantly changing—no two stimuli, and no two states of consciousness, are ever identical. Third, it is sensibly continuous in that there are no breaks in it; even though it is constantly changing, it remains fundamentally one chain. Fourth, it always deals with objects independent of itself, namely reality (note the similarity to Brentano's immanent objectivity). Finally, consciousness is selective: at a given time, the stream concerns itself with one aspect of awareness more than with another (a formulation reminiscent of Wundt's position on the focus of consciousness).

His psychology is not a true system, in the Wundtian sense. What James did was to give a detailed and critical report of the German work, and to use much of it to develop his own thoughts. Although his summary of the new German psychology was carefully prepared, thorough, and fair, he did not really like the work, but considered it dry, pedantic, and just plain dull. His interest in process rather than content, his analysis of habit, of emotion, and of the stream of consciousness, exemplified his functionalism, as contrasted with the German structuralism. Perhaps James can be considered the first true functionalist.

### James's Philosophy, His Laboratory, and His Students

James was interested in religious experience, and he was also fascinated by the occult phenomena of psychical research. In philosophy he was an interactionistic dualist, held a neorealistic position in epistemology, and espoused pragmatism when it comes to truth: that is true which works, as long as it works, and until something that works better comes along. Pragmatism has had a tremendous impact on modern philosophical thought.

There is some controversy about whether James or Wundt had the first laboratory of psychology; James did use a room for psychological demonstrations as early as 1875, a full four years before the formal existence of Wundt's research laboratory. But Wundt too had a demonstration laboratory in 1875. Wundt did found the first *research* laboratory for experimental psychology.

All in all, James played a major role in American psychology, largely through his writings, but also through his students, among the more influential of whom were James R. Angell, Mary W. Calkins, William Healy, Boris Sidis, Edward L. Thorndike, Robert S. Woodworth, and Robert M. Yerkes.

## OTHER AMERICAN PSYCHOLOGISTS OF THE TURN OF THE CENTURY

Most of James's contemporaries, and those who came right after him, studied abroad, and helped bring back the new psychology. Let us very briefly consider a few of the more significant ones.

### Hall and Sanford

G. Stanley Hall (1844–1924) studied at Bonn, Berlin, and Leipzig; if one omits James's demonstration laboratory at Harvard, Hall founded the first United States laboratory at Johns Hopkins in 1883. Thereafter he went to Clark University, as President. He started the *American Journal of Psychology*, edited the *Pedagogical Seminary* (which later became the *Journal of Genetic Psychology*), and also started the *Journal of Applied Psychology*. His interests were very broad; he was one of the first to devote much attention to individual differences. Using a light literary style similar to that of James, he wrote books on adolescence and on old age; he was also among the first to use the questionnaire method for psychological investigations, a method pioneered by Francis Galton. We shall return to Hall and his role in the founding of the American Psychological Association later in the chapter.

Hall turned over the Hopkins Laboratory to Edmund Clark Sanford (1859–1924), a close associate of Edwin Bradford Titchener's. It was Sanford who published the first laboratory manual of experimental psychology in the world.

### Ladd and Scripture

George Trumbull Ladd (1842–1921), at Yale, wrote the first text on physiological psychology in English in 1887; this work, later revised by Robert S. Woodworth, who had been James McKeen Cattell's student, continued to be influential for many decades.

Edward Wheeler Scripture (1864–1943), a brilliant experimentalist, studied with Wundt but also heard Ebbinghaus lecture; Ladd brought him to Yale to head the psychology laboratory there. He did extensive experimental work on reaction time, audition, and phonetics. Even though not very many students were introduced to the new psychology in his laboratory, the output of the laboratory was very great. For the ten years Scripture was at Yale a large annual volume, *The Yale Studies,* served as the publication outlet for this work. After having established himself so well at Yale, late in his career Scripture took off with his secretary for Europe, obtained an M.D., and then became Professor of Phonetics at the University of Vienna.

### Seashore and Baldwin

Carl Emil Seashore (1866–1949), born in Sweden, took his degree under Scripture at Yale, and then started the laboratory at the University of Iowa. (When he came to the United States he Americanized his name; it had been Sjöstrand.) It was from Scripture that he obtained his interest in psychology in general and in music in particular—for many years he was well known for his tests of musical ability. During Seashore's tenure as professor and then later as graduate dean at Iowa, the large number of 269 Ph.D.s were granted in psychology.

James Mark Baldwin (1861–1934) established a psychology laboratory at Toronto and then another at Princeton. He started several journals: the *Psychological Review,* the *Psychological Index* (a forerunner of *Psychological Abstracts*), and *Psychological Monographs.* He also published a major dictionary of philosophy and psychology. Much interested in the psychological development of the child and of the human race, he advocated the evolutionary notion that ontogeny recapitulates phylogeny; that is, that each child, in his development, repeats the development of the human race.

### Cattell, Jastrow, and Münsterberg

James McKeen Cattell (1860–1944) was an aggressive teacher, organizer, and editor; some 300 students, including E. L. Thorndike, R. S. Woodworth, and S. I. Franz, among others, took their Ph.D.s with him. He started the *Psychological Review* with Baldwin. After a few other appointments, he settled at Columbia; the remarkable breadth of his interests is shown by the fact that he edited *Popular Science Monthly,* the *Scientific Monthly, Science, School and Society,* and *The American Naturalist,* at various times. He began the Psychological Corporation, important in applied psychology in later years. In addition to his promotional activity, he also engaged in research, chiefly in individual differences, reaction time, and psychophysics.

Joseph Jastrow (1863–1944) directed the Wisconsin laboratory. Having obtained his Ph.D. from Hall, Jastrow did extensive research in psychophysics. He also popularized psychology in several books: one on Freud, another on irrational beliefs, and still another on general psychology.

Hugo Münsterberg (1863–1916) was brought by James to Harvard to head the experimental laboratory; James felt obliged to develop a laboratory at Harvard, even though he himself did not feel up to it. Münsterberg had been a brilliant experimentalist in Germany, but once in the United States turned his talents primarily to industrial and applied psychology, writing texts on law, industry, and national character.

### The Founding of Laboratories

Many laboratories were founded during the last two decades of the nineteenth century. There was the Harvard laboratory in the late seventies under James, and the Johns Hopkins laboratory founded by Hall in 1883. The founding of psychological laboratories in North America was only a few years behind similar events in Europe. In 1891 Frank Angell established the laboratory at Cornell, and in 1892 Ladd and Scripture founded the Yale laboratory, and Baldwin founded one at Toronto. The next year Baldwin founded one at Princeton. Virtually every major university had its laboratory within the next few decades.

The busy founding of laboratories, and the translation and writing of texts by teachers who were trained abroad, made the early leaders feel that they were following the German tradition. However, a change was gradually taking place, particularly in Chicago, leading to functionalism and eventually to behaviorism. Somehow the new psychology transplanted to the American continent soon took on a very different flavor, much more appropriate to the United States Ortgeist.

## THE FOUNDING AND DEVELOPMENT OF THE AMERICAN PSYCHOLOGICAL ASSOCIATION

Quite early in the period of development and growth of American psychology, the discipline institutionalized itself. The American Psychological Association (APA) was founded in 1892. By that year American psychology was leaving its cocoon, transmuted from a moralistic, philosophical, Puritanical inchworm into an exciting, soaring, self-consciously experimental creature.

In 1892 the student could pick up books like George Trumbull Ladd's *Elements of Physiological Psychology,* James Mark Baldwin's *Handbook of Psychology,* John Dewey's *Psychology,* and of course William James's huge *Principles of Psychology* (or its briefer version, which was published that year). All of these had been published within the preceding decade, and all of them presented the "new" psychology, most of it imported from Germany, and imbued with the German Ortgeist. It was not a pure import, though, but was already beginning to be contaminated by the peculiarly American functionalist orientation, and was becoming distinctively different from its parent version across the Atlantic—less ponderous, less systematic, more tolerant, and with somewhat different foci.

Who were the midwives at APA's birth, and how did the association get founded? Then, as always, there were the promoters, the organizers. Certainly one of the candidates most worthy of some such title was Granville

Stanley Hall, APA's first president, whom we met a few pages earlier. At his invitation, according to several standard historical sources, a select small group of seven prominent psychologists convened at Clark University on July 8, 1892, to help found the American Psychological Association. The delegates, who appointed themselves to APA's governing body, the Council, were Hall, then president of Clark University; G. S. Fullerton of the University of Pennsylvania, who was another early officer of the association; William James of Harvard; the laboratory founder James Mark Baldwin, who at the time was at Toronto; Joseph Jastrow of the University of Wisconsin, who a short five years before had received the first American Ph.D. specifically in psychology; G. T. Ladd of Yale, who was to become APA's second president; and James McKeen Cattell of Columbia University, who in 1888 had been appointed to the first professorship specifically in psychology anywhere in the world.

At least this was the composition of the group according to several sources; that there is a bit of confusion about what actually happened is shown by the claim of some other reliable sources that James was in Switzerland at the time; by some articles in the 1943 *Psychological Review,* in which it was asserted that Cattell and Jastrow both claimed that they were not present at that historic July meeting after all; and by E. G. Boring's preface to the 1967 APA convention guide, which avers that Sanford, Burnham, Fullerton, Nichols, Bryan, and Jastrow were there. E. R. Hilgard presented still another version at the 1967 APA convention. It seems that James was there and was not there; Cattell was there and was not there; Jastrow was there and was not there; and the same goes for Baldwin, Sanford, Nichols, Bryan, Burnham, and possibly still others. By exclusion, at least Hall and Fullerton were there. How hard it is really to pin something down in history! At any rate, whoever his colleagues were on that date, it seems that founder Hall founded APA in his study at Clark University on July 8, 1892.

Somewhat contradictory sources indicate that the original seven elected some twenty-odd additional charter members, such as Angell, Scripture, Witmer, and others, whose names are no longer so familiar; before the first regular annual meeting, held December 27, 1892, five more were added, including Hugo Münsterberg and Edward Bradford Titchener, both of whom came to America's shores earlier in the year.

Like many other scientific associations to this day, then, APA originally met during Christmas vacation. In 1892 when, at Fullerton's invitation, the first meeting was held in Philadelphia at the University of Pennsylvania, there were 31 members. Hall of course was elected president, since the idea of an APA had been his; for his presidential address he chose the title "The History and Prospects of Experimental Psychology in America." According to one source, a total of six papers were read; according to another, seventeen studies were presented; and according to still another, twelve members read papers.

Annual dues were set at $3, but in 1904 they were reduced to $1 because the Association's surplus had become too unwieldy. It was not until 1919, some fifteen years later, that they were raised again, to $2; then in 1923 they went to $5, in 1936 to $10. By the late 1960s they were $45 a year. But membership rose even more dramatically than dues—from 31 in 1892 to 375 in 1917, twenty-five years later. It went to over 3,000 a quarter of a century after that, in 1942, and to some 26,000 in 1967. Membership almost multiplied by 10 every twenty-five years. At this rate, one might guess at over 200,000 in 1992; membership should break a million by early in the twenty-first century, and APA should have a billion members before the century is over. To make a slight variation on a projection that E. G. Boring undertook in the 1950s, if the APA continues to grow at the rate it did during the first three-quarters of a century of its existence, by sometime in the twenty-second century there should be more psychologists than people in the world.

A formal constitution was adopted in 1894, when APA met at Princeton, with William James as president. According to published, presumably trustworthy records, 22 members attended this meeting, and a total of 38 members had paid their dues. The entire Constitution took up only 26 printed lines in the published proceedings in the *American Journal of Psychology*. Article I, in its entirety, read as follows: *"Object. The object of the association is the advancement of psychology as a science.* Those are eligible for membership who are engaged in this work." Articles II, III, and IV dealt with the Council, Officers, and dues, respectively, the fifth with what was essentially a local arrangements committee, Article VI with the printing of the proceedings, and the seventh and final article concerned amendments to the constitution. It was brief and to the point, far briefer than the document behind the governance of the vastly larger APA in the second half of the twentieth century, whose bylaws take up eight double-column pages of small type.

At the third annual meeting, which lasted from 10: 30 in the morning on December 27 to 4: 30 in the afternoon of the next day, the Secretary-Treasurer, James McKeen Cattell, reported that receipts, including a prior balance of $69.50, totaled $191.10; expenditures were $63.93, leaving a balance in APA's treasury of $127.17. Eighteen papers were presented at that convention. Among them was one by Sanford on apparatus, another by Cattell on the distribution of exceptional ability, studies on pain by several writers, a report on foveal nightblindness by Christine Ladd-Franklin, and of course James's presidential address.

How did people let others know what they were doing, if they *did not* present a paper at APA? For one thing, there was much informal correspondence. But publication was also an active medium. Some published in *Mind,* edited in England, and some in Wundt's *Philosophische Studien*; occasionally such journals as the *Educational Review,* the *Journal of*

*Comparative Neurology,* and the *Philosophical Review* carried articles by psychologists. A major outlet was the *American Journal of Psychology,* but William James and several others considered it too much a house organ for Hall and his Clark colleagues, and did not hold it in very high regard. Yet in several respects Hall was quite conscientious in his editing of the *AJP*—he tried to publish exhaustive abstracts and summaries of the entire psychological literature of the world in it, just as he tried similar exhaustive summaries of the literature in education and childhood in his *Pedagogical Seminary.*

As we have indicated before, the psychological scene during APA's infancy was of course largely imported from Germany; most of the important names of the day had studied overseas. But the United States, too, had its own laboratories, was developing its own textbooks, and had its own journals. The mental testing movement was beginning, primarily through Cattell's interest, but there were no clinical psychologists or psychological clinics as yet, although Hall did teach psychology to psychiatrists at Worcester State Hospital for a number of years from 1889 on. (What with the presidency of Clark, his books, his journals, his research, his teaching, and his involvement in APA, one can only wonder where Hall obtained his prodigious energy.) The APA was founded by excited, deeply involved men who considered themselves scientists and pioneers, on the frontiers of the new scientific psychology.

Some numbers mentioned earlier indicate how APA grew and prospered. Its character both changed and did not change. Although it owned no journals in 1892, by 1942 it owned 6, and by 1967 it owned over a dozen. These acquisitions clearly were consistent with Article I of the constitution adopted in 1894. Less consistent with it were the growing incursions of professionalism which led to a formal split, later somewhat precariously healed again, among the ranks of psychologists. APA was at first a scientific organization, but by the latter half of the twentieth century it was clearly less so. It became a scientific *and* a professional association, an amalgamation of the earlier American Psychological Association and of the American Association for Applied Psychology, which separated from and then rejoined APA during the second quarter of the twentieth century. By the 1960s, APA was more professional than scientific; for instance, the journals, rather than being subsidized by APA out of member dues, as one might think would be suggested by the spirit of the 1894 constitution, were priced so that income exceeded expenses, with the result that the scientific publishing ventures in effect subsidized the other activities of the APA's mammoth centralized operation, the large majority of whose remaining budget went to such not directly scientific endeavors as legislative contacts, professional affairs, and the concerns of the Board of Directors, the office of the Executive Officer, and the Business Affairs of the Association.

In 1930 the first regional associations, the Eastern Psychological Association and the Rocky Mountain Psychological Association, were affiliated with APA; soon other regional associations were founded, affiliated with APA, and flourished: the Western Psychological Association, the Midwestern Psychological Association, the Southwestern Psychological Association, the Southeastern Psychological Association, and the Southern Society for Philosophy and Psychology. By 1939 ten state associations had affiliated; by the 1960s almost all of the states had organizations affiliated with APA, and were represented on the Council of Representatives. The primary appeal of the state associations, for readily understood reasons, was to practitioners, rather than to academics. In 1892 almost all APA members were academics; by the middle of the twentieth century the academic was a minority member. Most states had certification or licensure of psychologists by the middle of the twentieth century, and at the national level the American Board of Examiners in Professional Psychology conducted thorough examinations for practitioners of clinical, counseling, and industrial psychology.

Professionalization was, of course, not the only difference between 1892 American psychology and American psychology in the latter part of the twentieth century, although it may have been the most visible one. In 1892, as has been said several times, U.S. psychology was primarily German; since the 1920s world psychology has been centered in the United States. The early APA annual budgets were of the order of $100, whereas by the 1960s they were over $3 million, and APA owned a new office building in the nation's capital. Psychology, at the national level and also at the institutional level, had become big business. In 1892 American psychology was a few dozen interested people; by three-quarters of a century later it was a powerful political force, composed of over 25,000 individuals, with local, state, and national influence.

As we shall elaborate in Part III, since 1892 the age of the great schools of psychology came and went—structuralism, functionalism, gestalt, and others—but later in the twentieth century there were different schools, some new, some not so new: factor analysis and psychoanalysis, existentialism and computerism, and at least one contemporary school, the Skinnerian, was formally enshrined as an APA division. The operationist revolution opened up areas to empirical research which the founders of APA could not have dreamed of—the scope of problems investigated empirically today is vastly greater than that which could be studied in 1892; it has become possible to measure motivation, meaning, minute currents in neural tissue, subtle aspects of interpersonal interaction, and myriads of other things which were unheard of as measurements seventy-five, fifty, twenty-five, or even ten years earlier. The contents of the APA convention guides in recent years show the vast diversity of what people who call themselves psychologists are doing more than three-quarters of a century after APA was born. Qualitatively there are, to be sure, papers on several problems and areas similar to those their ancestors were working on, but there is also much that could not have been seen in an APA program in the 1890s—some of it scientific, much of it professional. Quantitatively there are typically about one hundred times more program items included in APA conventions nowadays than were presented at an 1890s APA meeting.

There are other ways in which American psychology changed from the day of APA's founding to the time of the present writing, some of which we have already touched on and some of which will be considered in greater detail in Part III. One could point to the mental measurements movement, the interdisciplinary ideology, the prodigious growth in research grant support, movements to establish certification and to lobby for licensure, the proliferation of miniature theoretical models, the emphasis on quantification, the publication explosion, the mushrooming of new APA divisions, and still other developments.

Doubtless the tireless Hall would have been in accord with these directions and overjoyed at the status of APA, and of American psychology as it is today. Clearly, psychology has arrived; it is in. The science has grown prodigiously. Psychologists have something to practice, or at least (even with much necessary information concerning validity still lacking) practice it anyway, and the public demand for practitioners far exceeds the supply. There are thousands of practitioners, thousands of teachers, thousands of researchers. Where Hall would have been enthusiastic, what might William James have thought? Would his skeleton turn over in its grave or, perhaps because of his functionalist flair, would his bones sit up and take notice? Unfortunately—perhaps fortunately—we shall never know.

## SUMMARY OF PART II

Wilhelm Wundt, great systematizer, was influenced by the German Zeitgeist of the middle of the nineteenth century, which had been developing in the preceding century. Leibnitz's views on apperception and Wolff's psychology set the stage. Herbart's mathematical psychology, J. Müller's physiological work and Weber's experimentation in sensation, as well as Helmholtz's many scientific contributions, helped make the time ripe for Fechner to invent psychophysics. It was Wundt in the last decades of the nineteenth century who personified the new experimental psychology, with his detailed, logical, dry, systematic views, his active laboratory, and his many students. Wundt's structuralism took the limelight from Franz Brentano's act psychology, Stumpf's phenomenological work, and G. E. Müller's devoted experimentation, which nevertheless helped mold the new science of psychology. The physiologist Hering and the physicist Mach, both of whom contributed to the growing field of sensation and perception, also helped shape the new psychology. Külpe, the leader of the Würzburg school, questioned some of Wundt's systematic assumptions, with his own and his students' influential work on imageless thought, and Hermann Ebbinghaus made the study of learning and memory quantitative and experimental.

The new German psychology was experimental, elementistic, and associationistic; the chief method was introspective, although other techniques—memorization, reaction time, and so forth—were also being developed. It made much reference to physiology, and concentrated particularly on receptive processes. Vitalism was out and scientific materialism was in, and quantification had become an end in itself. It was mostly a psychology of mental content, but the seeds of an act psychology were also sprouting—in Brentano's formulations and in the Darwinian evolutionary psychology of Galton and others.

American psychology before William James came on the scene had been moralistic and philosophical. James, soon joined in his task by many other Americans who had gone to Leipzig to study with Wundt, carried the new psychology to the United States, where it took on a different, more functional, flavor. James stressed the role of habit, developed a theory of emotion, and presented an influential description of the stream of consciousness. American psychology grew rapidly; many laboratories of experimental psychology were founded in the United States in the last two decades of the nineteenth century. Within a few short years the new approach was firmly entrenched in American psychology, and psychology was institutionalized in the United States with the founding of the American Psychological Association in 1892. The APA gradually grew and prospered, until by the latter half of the twentieth century it was a huge organization, partly scientific and largely professional, publishing many journals and sponsoring mammoth conventions for the exchange of psychological knowledge.

# PART III

# Psychology in the Twentieth Century

# 9

# The Age
# of Schools

The psychology of the twentieth century was a direct outgrowth of the trends we considered in Parts I and II. Several of these coalesced during the first decades of the twentieth century into cohesive schools, but by the middle of the century the schools had lost their function as foci for research and for theoretical controversy. By the time the age of schools had come to an end, there had developed a general acceptance of the empirical method, which was extended to nearly all corners of psychology's subject matter, and which had an increasingly quantitative orientation. Psychology also left the university to enter the field of public affairs, and psychologists engaged in great numbers in clinical practice and other service work.

## THE GREAT SCHOOLS OF PSYCHOLOGY

During the second decade of the twentieth century, five major points of view became foci for psychologists' dedicated theoretical commitment; each of these schools had its own particular convictions about the definition of psychology, the task of psychology, and the methods appropriate to the fulfillment of that task. For a while each seemed to be convinced it was right, and everybody else was wrong. We shall examine them here very briefly and comparatively by way of introduction, before discussing each a bit more fully in the next five chapters.[1]

[1] It might be worthwhile to read the present chapter twice, first to obtain a preliminary overview of the schools and then once more, after having read the next five chapters, to help pull the material together. The two summary tables included in this chapter are apt to be more meaningful after one is somewhat acquainted with the details of the schools' positions.

Wundt's and Titchener's *structuralism* wanted to find out about the content of the mind and studied it by introspection. *Functionalism* was more concerned with adaptation—that is, What are the various activities of the mind for? There were two centers of functionalism, the Chicago School of Angell, Carr, Dewey, and Mead, and the Columbia School of Cattell, Thorndike, and Woodworth. *Behaviorism* insisted that psychology should study behavior, and not experience; objective experimentation was the only legitimate method. The leading early figure here was Watson; more recent behaviorists included Hull, Guthrie, Spence, and Skinner. The *gestalt psychologists,* Koffka, Köhler, and Wertheimer, and later Goldstein and Lewin, disagreed with the other three schools; they maintained that both experience and behavior are legitimate areas for the psychologist to study, and that he should use whatever method is appropriate to the problem—as long as he is careful to avoid an artificial or arbitrary cutting up of the phenomenon on which he is working. The fifth major school, *psychoanalysis,* did not really flourish in experimental psychology; the first four were crossing swords with one another, but psychoanalysis was in a different arena. The pioneer here was Freud; among the more influential later theorists were Jung and Adler. Psychoanalysis, using the methods of free association and of dream analysis, attempted to understand the fundamental processes of the conscious and unconscious mind, and the dynamic forces composing the personality.

## SOME ISSUES ON WHICH THE SCHOOLS DIFFERED

Table 1 presents a capsule overview of where the five schools stood on some of the important questions of the day. As the first row in the table indicates, structuralism and behaviorism attempted to reduce behavior to fundamental elements (mental elements in the one case, stimuli and responses in the other), while the gestalt approach was against an atomistic, elementistic approach and for the structural analysis of naturally occurring wholes, arguing that the whole is different from the sum of its parts; functionalism attempted reduction to adaptive processes as well as just to structural elements. Psychoanalysis did not really have much to say on this issue, and yet it did try to get at processes via a kind of mental elements or problem experiences: What areas, what particular experiences, are disturbing to the person?

Secondly, the schools differed on whether psychology should be subjective or objective. Structuralism, early functionalism, and psychoanalysis were all frankly mentalistic; but behaviorism was explicitly antimentalistic, while gestaltists were willing to accept mentalistic or behavioral information, depending upon the nature of the problem being investigated.

# TABLE 1

The Schools of Psychology and What They Stood For

| School (and representative adherents) | Structuralism (Wundt, Titchener) | Functionalism (Angell, Carr, Thorndike, Woodworth) | Behaviorism (Watson, Hunter, Hull) | Gestalt Psychology (Wertheimer, Kaffka, Kohler) | Psychoanalysis (Freud, Jung, Adler) |
|---|---|---|---|---|---|
| Unit of study | Mental elements | Mental elements and adaptive processes | S–R elements | Antielements (natural wholes or gestalten) | Elements and processes |
| Subjective or objective? | Mentalism (subjective) | Mostly mentalism (subjective) | Antimentalism (objective) | Both subjective and objective | Mentalism (subjective) |
| What should psychology study? | Content | Mostly function, but also content | Content and function | Content and function | Content and function |
| Preferred method | Introspection | Introspection; later, behavior observation, too | Behavior observation | Phenomenology and behavior observation | Free association |
| Purpose: pure or applied? | Pure | Pure and applied | Pure and applied | Mostly pure | More applied than pure |
| Nomothetic or idiographic? | Global laws (nomothetic) | Some individual differences (idiographic) but mostly global laws | Both | Both | More individual differences than global laws |
| Physiological explanation | Physiological hookups | Physiological why or what for | Physiological hookups | Physiological fields | Biological drives? |

95

Structuralism maintained that psychology should study the content of mental experience; functionalism was more interested in the functioning or operation of these contents. The schools were interested in both.

The method of choice of the structuralists and the early functionalists was systematic introspection, while the behaviorists argued for the exclusive legitimacy of the observation of behavior; gestalt psychologists used phenomenology, or "naive introspection," and also observation of the behavior of both animals and people. The psychoanalysts had their own particular form of "introspection"—free association.

While the structuralists, and to some extent the gestaltists, were primarily interested in trying to develop an understanding of psychological processes for their own sake, functionalism extended its inquiry to educational psychology and other applied problems: What do the various psychological processes achieve for the organism? Behaviorism was concerned both with "pure" problems and with the application of psychological knowledge to real-life situations; psychoanalysis focused mostly on the applied problem of helping the troubled individual, but also tried to understand mental processes for their own sake.

While structuralism wanted to establish global laws that would hold for all people (what Gordon Allport has called the nomothetic approach), functionalism was also interested in individual differences. The remaining three schools worked on both, with psychoanalysis somewhat more concerned with attempts to understand the psychological processes within particular individuals (Allport's idiographic approach) than with establishing general laws.

All five schools felt that psychology could profit from knowledge of physiology, but in different ways. The structuralists and behaviorists looked for physiological hookups, or connections, to account for psychological or behavioral events, whereas the functionalists were more concerned with the physiological adaptive processes presumed to underlie behavior. The gestalt psychologists, too, sought physiological explanations of psychological events, but looked to neurological and electrical fields rather than to the neural circuitry of the structuralists and behaviorists. The psychoanalysts did not make the same kind of explanatory use of physiological concepts as did the other four schools, but held that the roots of behavior and experience lay in powerful biological drives.

## HOW THE SCHOOLS RELATED TO THE EIGHT TRENDS

Table 2 attempts to show in a nutshell how the five schools were related to the five scientific and the three philosophical trends that we considered in Part I. The entries in the table are to be read as though each cell raised a question. Thus in the upper left cell, the question would be, Did

**TABLE 2**

How the Schools of Psychology Exemplified the Eight Trends

| | Structuralism | Functionalism | Behaviorism | Gestalt Psychology | Psychoanalysis |
|---|---|---|---|---|---|
| Physiology | A bit, for explanation | Yes: adaptive processes | Yes: neural hookups | Yes: brain model | Not really |
| Biology | Not really | Yes: strongly evolutionary | Yes: behavior and evolution | A little: living systems are gestalten | Somewhat: the id drives |
| Atomism | Yes: mental elements | Yes: mental elements | Yes: S–R bonds | No: antielementism | Maybe: traumatic experiences |
| Quantification | Yes, some | Yes, some | Yes | Yes | No |
| Laboratories | Yes | Yes | Yes | Yes | No |
| Critical empiricism | Yes | Yes | Yes | Yes | Yes, loosely |
| Associationism | Yes | Yes | Yes | No: antiassociationistic | Maybe: free association |
| Scientific materialism | Some | Yes: study of the organism | Strongly: objectivism | Yes: brain model | Not really |

structuralism manifest the physiological trend? In the fourth cell down in that column, the question would be, Did structuralism manifest the trend toward quantification? The answer to the first question, as the table indicates, is a qualified positive in that structuralism did hold that physiological concepts can serve an explanatory end. To the second question the answer is again a qualified Yes, because although there was some attempt at quantification, there was also much nonquantified concern with the accurate qualitative description of the mental elements yielded in careful introspection.

Structuralism, then, displayed the physiological and quantitative trends to some degree. It was not strongly biological, but was atomistic and associationistic in its interest in mental elements and their compounding. The emphasis on experimental work accounts for the conclusion that the laboratory founding and critical empiricist traditions too were evident in structuralism. Finally, although the structuralists tried to pin down psychological processes, the strongly mentalistic flavor of structuralism precludes the judgment that it was very scientifically materialistic.

Functionalism displayed all eight of the trends. Its evolutionary interest in adaptive processes exemplified its biological and physiological antecedents. It was empirical and laboratory-oriented, associationistic, and elementistic. Somewhat more quantitative, perhaps, than structuralism, it was basically materialistic in its concentration on the organism.

Behaviorism too evidenced all eight trends, being most insistent of all the schools in regard to scientific materialism: objectivity was its fetish. Thus the behaviorist's elements were not the mental ones of the structuralist and early functionalist, but the behavioral ones of stimuli and responses; the question of association was recast into the language of conditioning, and neural hookups were assumed to underlie the behavioral ones. Behaviorism had a biological, evolutionary tinge, and strongly advocated quantified laboratory investigation.

Gestalt psychology's very existence as a separate school depended on its objection to two of the eight trends. It was militantly antiatomistic and antiassociationistic; wholes, it held, are not composed of inert elements arbitrarily hooked together. Gestalt notions were also applied to the presumed operation of the brain and other living systems, so in its own somewhat different way the gestalt movement exemplified the physiological, biological, and scientific materialist interests of preceding times. As dedicated to quantitative, controlled laboratory studies as behaviorism, it therefore also fitted into the traditions of quantification, critical empiricism, and laboratory founding.

As for psychoanalysis, the basic difference between it and the remaining schools shows up in the fact that none of the eight trends really characterized it directly. Perhaps the libidinal drive could be seen as in some sense biological, but psychoanalysis is not physiological, nor scientifically materialistic. The laboratory atmosphere was essentially alien to it, as was quantification. Possibly one could argue that the traumatic experiences of childhood, responsible for later pathology, might in some sense be seen as functionally elementary experiences, thus slightly reflecting the atomistic trend. Comparably, one might stretch the associationistic tradition to encompass free association, using it to trace the associational network in an analysand's mind, but the parallel may be little more than verbal. To the extent that psychoanalysts did try to observe without bias, rather than just spinning speculative, deductive webs, psychoanalysis might be interpreted to have been at least tinged with the spirit of critical empiricism.

## THE DECLINE OF THE SCHOOLS

During the 1920s all five schools vigorously pursued their respective goals, although structuralism and functionalism were already beginning to recede into history at the end of that decade. By the middle of the twentieth century, the gestalt movement had lost its identity as a major separate school, structuralism was essentially dead, and functionalism no longer existed as a movement; but much of American psychology by then was tinged with functionalist thought. Only behaviorism and psychoanalysis continued as powerful schools. All in all, it was primarily the second and third decades of the twentieth century that can be considered the age of schools; as was mentioned in the preceding chapter, though, there were vestiges of a "school" tendency in the middle of the century, as in Carl Rogers' client-centered counseling (a major rallying point among clinical psychologists), in the factor analysis of workers like Raymond B. Cattell and Hans-Jurgen Eysenck, or in the objective behavioristics of the followers of B. F. Skinner.

In the 1930s, 1940s, and 1950s, people became generally somewhat more tolerant, perhaps because of the growth and evident success of psychology; they became less insistent about legislating what other psychologists can or cannot do. Unquestioning devotion to and reverence for figures like Wundt, Titchener, and Watson subsided substantially. There was a growing recognition that maybe the other fellow's work was not totally useless, after all; maybe different viewpoints, each in its own way, do have something valuable to contribute to the understanding of psychological problems. Although the middle of the twentieth century still witnessed occasional outbursts of people telling other people how they should go about their work, a kind of "live and let live" philosophy seemed gradually to pervade the Zeitgeist. The prevailing attitude became that my road to the truth is, of course, better than yours, but you have a right to follow your misguided approach, and, who knows, it may even yield something worthwhile. Nothing is apt to be lost by attacking a problem simultaneously from several different angles and with several different methods, or by attacking different problems.

# 10

# Structuralism

Wundt attempted to understand the structure of the mind, and to develop a rigorous psychological system. One of his most distinguished students, Edward Bradford Titchener (1867–1927), carried on the systematic, almost authoritarian Wundtian tradition, bringing it to the United States. There it never took firm root, and it seems to have died with Titchener, so we can summarize it here quite briefly.

## TITCHENER

Titchener developed the fundamental distinction, made earlier by James, between structuralism and functionalism; structuralism is curious about the "is," whereas functionalism wonders about the "is for." Titchener called himself and Wundt structuralists; he was a highly systematic disciple of Wundt—as Boring put it, he outWundted Wundt. Titchener had a tight group of devoted followers, but his influence did not extend far beyond this group, nor did structuralism live long after Titchener's death—although he did leave important students, among them Karl Dallenbach and Edwin G. Boring, and important students of students, such as Boring's student S. S. Stevens.

Born in England, and British in his habits until his death, Titchener studied philosophy at Oxford, then went to Leipzig in 1890. Obtaining his Ph.D. from Wundt in 1892, he went in the same year to Cornell, and stayed there until his death thirty-five years later. Accepting Wundtian structuralism completely and without question, he brought it to the United States almost without modification.

Somewhat isolated from other Americans, Titchener did have a few close friends among his students. He was not particularly active in organized American psychology; although he did join the American Psychological Association, he soon engaged in a controversy about reaction times with Baldwin, who was somewhat brusque in his criticisms of Titchener, and Titchener then resigned from the APA. In 1904 he created his own society, a small, closed group, largely composed of his own students; he wanted to call it "the Fechner club," but the charter members would not go along with that, and it never had a real name until after Titchener's death. People referred to it as "the Experimentalists" or even "Titchener's Experimentalists." Named the Society of Experimental Psychologists in 1928, it has been a formal, self-conscious, select fraternity and continues to flourish as of the present writing. A highly ritualistic man, Titchener always lectured in his Oxford master's gown; his lectures were very carefully prepared, and his entire staff attended all his lectures. They filed dutifully into the lecture room before the professor entered, and sat in special seats, regularly reserved for them, in the front of the room.

Titchener wrote a great deal, turning out a brief *Outline of Psychology* in 1896, and a *Primer of Psychology* in 1898. In 1901 he began publication of several manuals of experimental psychology; each manual was accompanied by a comprehensive instructor's guide. There was one manual for qualitative analysis, and a second for quantitative analysis; the somewhat pretentious parallel with chemistry is by no means accidental. By 1910 he had published an experimental psychology of feeling and emotion, and another on the thought processes; the latter, incidentally, provided a fair, balanced presentation of the research of Külpe and his Würzburg school, even though Titchener's own position was diametrically opposed to Külpe's. In the same year appeared the *Textbook of Psychology,* Titchener's most systematic work. About 1912 he began a still more systematic treatise, which appeared as four articles during Titchener's lifetime in the *American Journal of Psychology,* and which was published after Titchener's death as a book, edited by H. P. Weld, in 1929.

## TITCHENER'S STRUCTURALISM

Structuralism holds that psychological wholes are compounds of elements; psychology's task is to discover the elements and the manner in which they compound. One must begin with the atoms or elements; science goes from the part to the whole. The elements are conscious contents, mental contents. The method of choice is systematic introspection by highly trained observers.

Titchener divided psychology into human, animal, social, child, and abnormal psychology; in practice, however, he was sympathetic only to what he called human psychology: the real task of psychology is to understand the structure and content of the adult human mind, well-trained in systematic introspection. This preference of his was, it seems, shown in his and his coeditors' editing of the *American Journal of Psychology* in that all papers reporting studies on subjects other than adult humans were reputedly rejected.

The fact that Titchener was a dogmatic disciple of Wundt does not mean that he did not make a few innovations. For example, while the Wundtian elements were sensations, images, and feelings, Titchener renamed the third class: his elements were sensations, images (elements of memory), and affections. In Chapter 6 we indicated that Titchener modified Wundt's tridimensional theory of feelings (or affections).

Another elaboration was Titchener's vehement emphasis on the necessity of avoiding the "stimulus error"; introspective descriptions must be carefully limited to the contents of the experience being analyzed, and not be contaminated by knowledge of the nature of the stimulus responsible for the mental contents. Thus a proper psychological description of an apple must include material on its color, shape, smell, weight, taste, and the like; but it would be a mistake to call it an apple, which we know to be an edible fruit.

Related to concern about the stimulus error—in that avoidance of this error necessitates, according to Titchener, avoidance of meanings if we are to have genuine psychological descriptions of introspective material—is Titchener's fairly influential "context theory of meaning": each experience has an elemental core and a meaning-providing context. Perceptions have sensory cores and ideas have imaginal cores. The context can be sensory (as in the kinesthetic accentuation of rhythm) or imaginal (as in recalling the name of a familiar face). It is the associated context that gives meaning to any experience.

Psychology was conceived by Titchener to be the study of mind, which is the sum total of human experience considered as dependent upon the experiencing person. Psychology should strive to answer the what, the how, and the why. "What" is the task of analysis—into the simplest components; "why" is the task of synthesis of the complex out of the elements; and "how" is the question of the laws of connection of the elements, arrived at by analysis. Systematization and explanation occur via the nervous system; Titchener was a psychophysical parallelist, who argued that explanation via processes in the nervous system brings unity and coherence to the study of psychological processes: the description of mental contents alone is not enough. Physiological concepts, then, provide a kind of "how," an explanation and a systematic approach; but, Titchener commented, they do not "add one iota" to the introspective data, which are the primary data of psychology.

Titchener's Cornell laboratory was an active, exciting place to be in during Titchener's days there. The traditional Wundtian problems were being pursued zealously, and some students who were to be important in later years were deeply inspired by Titchener's rigorous enthusiasm. With Titchener's system, there seemed to be a possibility that another forty or fifty years of diligent research might bring psychology to the state of an essentially completed science—all the important problems would have been solved by that time, and only a little refined clean-up work would remain. Clearly, though, that is not how later psychology developed.

# 11

# Functionalism

Functionalism flourished primarily at two major universities: Chicago and Columbia. At Chicago it was an explicit and self-conscious system; at Columbia it was not at all systematically self-conscious, but was, rather, a kind of unconscious attitude. This attitude soon spread over most of America, which may be one reason why behaviorism—very self-conscious— soon displaced it, spreading rapidly from Johns Hopkins University all over the country. At both Chicago and Columbia the concern was with the "why" of experience and behavior, but for the functionalists this did not mean, as for Titchener, the synthesis of experience out of mental elements, but rather an examination of the adaptive functions of mind for the organism. The predecessors of the later functionalist movement, therefore, include not only James with his concern about the "what for," but also Brentano with his act psychology, Spencer and Darwin and their evolutionism, and Galton, among others.

## CHICAGO FUNCTIONALISTS

### Dewey

Well-known for his educational philosophy of "learning by doing," John Dewey (1859–1952) was most renowned as a philosopher and educational theorist, although many of his contributions were significant for psychology proper. He was at Chicago from 1894 until 1904, when he went to Columbia. He published a textbook of psychology and a small volume on thinking, both of which were influential; his book on thinking, *How We*

*Think,* viewed the process as an adaptation to a novel problematic situation. Thinking occurs if the organism is thwarted in its desires, and ceases when the desires are fulfilled.

Dewey's most significant contribution to psychology, however, is generally considered to be his 1896 article in the *Psychological Review* on the reflex arc concept. Dewey here was against elementism in psychology and physiology, and severely criticized the atomistic approaches of writings like William James's analysis of habits. Dewey argued that one cannot split up a piece of behavior into arcs, and the arcs into stimuli and responses; the distinction between a stimulus and a response, furthermore, is a purely functional one—one cannot have a response without a stimulus, and vice versa. The two are correlative, and the arc must be considered as a whole, a purposeful, adaptive, useful whole. Here Dewey anticipated the later thinking of the gestalt psychologists.

### Angell

James Rowland Angell (1869–1949) studied both abroad and under James at Harvard but never bothered to finish his Ph.D. His career, which included the supervision of many doctoral theses, demonstrated that one need not have those three letters after one's name to be creative, original, productive. He too arrived at Chicago in 1894. Remembered by his students as an impressive man who gave an excellent course in the history of psychology, Angell wrote a textbook in psychology which was much less philosophical than Dewey's. Its title was *Psychology: An Introductory Study of the Structure and Function of the Human Consciousness*; particularly in Chapter 1, it stressed the *function* of consciousness.

Angell was elected president of the American Psychological Association in 1906, and he chose "The Province of Functional Psychology" as the title for his presidential address. In this paper he distinguished sharply between structuralism and functionalism. Structuralism studies conscious content, whereas functionalism studies the operations of consciousness. Structuralism attempts analysis into elements, whereas functionalism is concerned with the nature and functions of mental processes, with emphasis on how these processes work. Functionalism conceives of consciousness not as just a passive receptacle for experience, but as engaged in "an adaptive reaction to a novel situation."

Angell had a successful academic career, and had a profound influence on many students, including the later functionalist Carr, the behaviorists John B. Watson, Walter S. Hunter, and Karl F. Muenzinger, and the pioneer industrial psychologist Walter van Dyke Bingham; his text was also very popular for a long time. As happens with many able academic men, he was persuaded to leave the laboratory and the study to undertake administrative work in his later years, serving as president of Yale University from 1921 to 1937.

### Carr and Mead

Harvey Carr (1873–1954) obtained his Bachelor's and Master's degrees at the University of Colorado, then went to Chicago, where he was to stay for the remainder of his professional life. He completed his Ph.D. degree under Angell in 1907, with a study on illusions. An accomplished experimentalist, Carr continued to study perception and animal behavior for many years, working with mazes, discrimination boxes, and problem boxes. Very much of an empiricist, he was relatively little concerned with theory, and he did not get around to publishing his textbook, based on notes he had used many years, until 1925: *Psychology: A Study of Mental Activity.* An unabashed pragmatist when it came to theory and practice, in his 1926 presidential address to the American Psychological Association Carr reflected that when he was dealing with animals, he was a behaviorist, but when dealing with humans, he was a mentalist.

Carr's important theoretical contributions to functionalism were mostly incidental by-products of his experimental work. Carr held that the subject matter of psychology is mental activity, and mental activity is adaptive ("the organism adapts"). Mental activity is manipulation of certain experiences in order to attain certain ends. Every adaptive act involves three aspects, according to Carr: there is a motivating stimulus, which provides direction; a sensory situation, which is perceived or cognized; and a response, which alters the situation in such a way that the motivating conditions are satisfied. Organisms never act randomly; behavior is always relevant to the situation; all behavior is motivated.

George Herbert Mead (1863–1931), though a professor of philosophy, gave courses and seminars in the scientific method in psychology, in social psychology, and in the psychology of language, and was closely associated with the functionalists in the psychology department at Chicago. Among his contributions was a functional definition of meaning: the meaning of an object depends on its function. Thus a pencil, for example, is a noise-maker, spear, bookmark, writing tool, and so forth, depending upon the way in which it is used.

### COLUMBIA FUNCTIONALISTS

At Chicago, functionalism grew out of structuralism, as imported from Germany and as reinterpreted by William James. Functionalism at Chicago served as the bridge between structuralism and behaviorism; the concern with the adaptive properties of behavior characteristic of the functionalists was taken over as a major concern of the behaviorists. Columbia functionalism also developed in the same directions. It started a little later than Chicago functionalism, and was soon strengthened by Dewey's coming to Columbia in 1904. At Columbia there was also James McKeen Cattell, very much interested in individual differences and in applied psychology, whom we have already encountered in Chapter 8; two other major figures were Thorndike and Woodworth.

### Thorndike

Edward L. Thorndike (1874–1949) was trained at Harvard and then Columbia. He undertook his dissertation research on animal intelligence, studying how dogs, cats, and chicks learned to get out of a puzzle box. (At Harvard, the authorities were leery of permitting smelly animals to be kept in the hallowed halls, so the preliminary research for Thorndike's doctoral thesis was done in the basement of William James's graciously offered Cambridge home.) Thorndike's Ph.D. thesis, submitted to Columbia, was published as a monograph in 1898. In it, he reported that he found a slow, continuous increase in the efficiency of behavior during problem solving, and argued that learning occurs mechanically, with the gradual elimination of wrong responses. Behavior in a new problem situation, he said, is initially random. The random behavior and its consequences lead eventually to mechanical connections between stimuli and responses; learning is by blind trial and error. This point of view led him to his highly influential formulation of the law of effect: that in a given stimulus situation any act followed by a satisfier will be stamped in, while any act followed by an annoyer will be stamped out. That is, reward stamps in the S-R connection or bond, and punishment stamps it out.

In 1932, shortly before his retirement, Thorndike proposed the "truncated" law of effect; experiments had shown that the function of punishment is not as straightforward as he had first thought—punishment does not weaken connections in the same way that reward strengthens them. Accordingly, he dropped the second half of the law concerning punishment.

Thorndike's approach is still central to the Ortgeist of the American psychology of learning; it has been extremely influential. The reinforcement formulations of Hull, Skinner, and Spence, to mention just a few important later workers, were essentially more sophisticated restatements of Thorndike's law of effect. His influence on the behaviorists suggests that one might consider him a behaviorist almost as readily as a functionalist.

Employed by Columbia immediately after his Ph.D., Thorndike was considered the outstanding psychologist at Teachers College there for many years. A forceful, down-to-earth man, Thorndike had many followers. He was one of the early great American experimental educational psychologists, and his doctrines dominated educational practice and the psychology of learning for decades. He was a very prolific man. Among his works were a 3-volume educational psychology (later condensed into one), and books on the theory of measurement, on learning, and on educational policy; after his retirement he went into sociology, writing on such issues as the characteristics of a good community. Throughout his career he called himself a connectionist, because he wanted to show how bonds between stimuli and responses are developed—a concern that he had acquired while working with James at Harvard, before his Ph.D.

### Woodworth

Robert Sessions Woodworth (1869–1962) had a long life and a long, distinguished career in psychology. He collaborated early on a book in physiological psychology with Ladd, and later produced his own editions. In 1901 he and Thorndike performed a famous experiment on transfer of training, defeating the educational philosophy of formal discipline, by demonstrating that mental skills are not, like muscles, strengthened by training, but that it is only identical elements that are transferred from one learning activity to another. Woodworth also wrote a widely read history of psychology (*Contemporary Schools of Psychology*) which he revised later and which came out in a third edition, with Mary Sheehan's coauthorship, shortly after Woodworth's death. His *Experimental Psychology* (first published in 1938 and later revised by Harold Schlosberg) proved to be the standard text in its field for several decades until it was replaced by Charles E. Osgood's equally monumental book in the same field in the early 1950s.

In much of his work, Woodworth's functional orientation led him to what he called a dynamic view, which emphasized the importance of motivation in the understanding of behavior, with such principles as that mechanisms may become drives. That is, well-trained patterns may carry with them their own motivation. He also argued that one must consider the organism's contribution to its behavior, and inserted the organism into the behaviorist's S-R formula, rewriting it S-O-R. His book, *Dynamic Psychology*, published late in his career, was a fitting capstone to his many contributions to his discipline. He was active and sprightly to the end.[1]

---

[1] The present writer remembers with pleasure and some degree of awe being among a group of Woodworth's students and interested followers walking between hotels at an APA convention which was held after Woodworth's ninetieth birthday. Most of us were huffing and puffing, having a hard time keeping up with the nonagenarian's pace, both intellectually and on foot.

## THE IMPACT OF FUNCTIONALISM

Early functionalism, then, concerned itself with mind in use—mind as an adaptive process. Chicago functionalism began within the introspective tradition, but especially at Columbia, later research concentrated on "the adaptive processes of the organism." Thus functionalism served as a bridge to behaviorism, placing great emphasis upon learning (an orientation that was to continue to be characteristic of later twentieth-century American psychology); it also greatly furthered the cause of applied psychology.

It might well be considered characteristic of functionalism that it followed its own precepts, adapting itself to the changing scene of psychology so efficiently that it adapted itself right out of existence as a separate school and merged successfully into mid-twentieth-century American psychology. It did its job so well that a functional orientation has continued to be a major hallmark of American psychology down to the time of the present writing.

# 12

# Behaviorism

## ANTECEDENTS OF BEHAVIORISM

While behaviorism perhaps can claim to rival functionalism as the most peculiarly American of the schools, its predecessors were Europeans rather than Americans. True, it was John B. Watson, very much an American, who popularized the school, but many others before him had propounded the doctrines that were later to become central to it. Elementism (atomism, reductionism) had been in the air for centuries, as was the concern with compounds (associationism); in later behaviorism, this took the form of an intense interest in discrimination and in conditioning, the most important early work on which was done in Russia (although the Russian work was not really discovered by the Americans until about 1913). The mentalistic associationism of early philosophers and psychologists was turned by the behaviorists into S-R associationism; antimentalistic biases had been around for a long time in the scientific materialism movement, and the emphasis upon objectivity had many antecedents.

### Scientific Materialism

Behaviorism fits perfectly into the tradition of scientific materialism. The influential evolutionary biologist Jacques Loeb, whom we encountered briefly in Chapter 4 as a later representative of this point of view, in 1890 published some of his work on tropistic, mechanical behavior in animals; in 1912 he published *The Mechanistic Conception of Life*, an outstanding restatement of scientific materialism in the tradition of Descartes and the

French materialists. Then there were the objective Russian physiologists or "reflexologists," particularly I. M. Sechenov (1829–1905), Ivan P. Pavlov (1849–1936), and Vladimir Bekhterev (1857–1927). As early as the 1860s, Sechenov was experimenting with reflexes, and maintaining that the proper way to study psychological processes was via the physiological investigation of reflexes.

Although Russian reflexology, then, began with Sechenov, it is Pavlov who is best known in this area. After winning the Nobel prize for his study of digestive secretions, he turned the attention of his laboratory to what he called conditional reflexes; almost everybody knows about his famous study of salivation in dogs. The prototypic experiment showed that an originally neutral stimulus, such as a bell, which does not produce salivation, will do so after repeated pairing of the bell and the presentation of food powder. Pavlov and his colleagues undertook extensive systematic experiments on this phenomenon, recognizing its importance for the objective analysis of psychic processes.

Bekhterev in 1910 published *Objective Psychology,* and a few years later a book on human reflexology; in both of these, he took a thoroughgoing antimentalistic position, and devoted himself solely to the description of behavior.

Then there was Max Meyer (1873–1967), a Swiss who obtained his Ph.D. from Stumpf and then immigrated to the United States, and who published in 1911 *The Fundamental Laws of Human Behavior,* in which behavior was defined in a completely objective fashion. In 1921 he published *The Psychology of the Other One,* in which he argued that in order to be objective, psychology must avoid all introspection and only make statements and observations concerning the behaviors of other people.

### McDougall

In Chapter 7, we mentioned William McDougall, an Englishman who settled in the United States. He published several important books early in the twentieth century; in 1912 appeared his *Psychology: The Study of Behaviour,* in which he asserted that psychology should not be the study of the mind, as in structuralism and in early functionalism, but rather the study of behavior. He proposed a purposive behaviorism or "hormic" psychology; behavior objectively demonstrates purpose; that is, behavior does not occur in a vacuum but aims at some specific goal. The similarity of this view to some of the tenets of act psychology and of functionalism shows how much the concern with adaptation was in the Zeitgeist. Its emphasis on purpose was also to be taken over, in modified form, by the later "purposive behaviorist" Edward C. Tolman and his students. As we indicated in

Chapter 7, though, McDougall took pains later to dissociate himself from what he considered the misguided behaviorism of Watson and his followers.

### Animal Behavior

Also leading into the development of behaviorism was the long tradition of interest in animal psychology in England, the United States, and elsewhere, which we examined briefly in Chapter 7. The study of animal behavior was particularly congenial to behaviorism because one cannot ask animals what their mental states are like and expect a coherent answer in one's own native language. If objective observations can be used to understand the psychological processes of animals, Watson was to ask later, why can't one do the same thing with human beings?

Among the important workers in this tradition were the tropists, like Loeb, and the workers under the Darwinian influence, like Romanes, Lloyd Morgan, Jennings, and Lubbock, whom we have briefly alluded to before. And of course there was Thorndike, with his 1898 *Animal Intelligence* (which came out in 1911 in a second edition). In 1901 W. S. Small of Clark University published the first study of the behavior of rats in a maze, introducing the maze method in the study of animal intelligence and learning; this method was to be used in thousands of experiments in subsequent decades. Robert M. Yerkes (1876–1956), a distinguished Harvard comparative psychologist who had a long, productive career, in 1907 published *The Dancing Mouse,* a report of a wide variety of experiments using discrimination apparatus, mazes, and problem boxes. This was but an early one of many significant contributions of Yerkes to the rapidly growing field of comparative psychology; he worked, among other species, with crabs, turtles, frogs, worms, pigs, doves, monkeys, and apes.

Titchener's first doctoral student, Margaret F. Washburn, published *The Animal Mind* in 1908; by that time she had become chairman of the psychology department at Vassar College. This book was very widely used, and went through four editions. The title of the book, incidentally, was a concession to structuralism and functionalism; it was concerned solely with animal *behavior.* Among the issues it discussed was the question of whether animals have minds, in the sense of memory images. It was this that led Carr later to suggest to his and Angell's student Walter S. Hunter that he study delayed reaction in order to measure symbolic processes objectively.

Watson, in his *Behavior: An Introduction to Comparative Psychology* (1914) surveyed much of the prior animal experimentation. Animal psychology has been and has remained a major interest of United States psychologists throughout the twentieth century. It is congenial to functionalism, as well as to behaviorism, because the observation of animal behavior almost inevitably requires attention to the use or function of the behavior or the act.

## WATSON

### Watson's Life and Work

John B. Watson (1878–1958), extreme, systematic, somewhat superficial, and very influential, was behaviorism's main popularizer. He obtained his Ph.D. in 1903 at Chicago, with a thesis in which he studied the function of the various sensory cues that rats use in learning to run through a maze. He eliminated one sensory modality after another, and found that the rats were, by and large, still able to run the maze reasonably well, showing that several modalities were simultaneously involved in the learning. Watson was put in charge of the animal laboratory at Chicago immediately after he obtained his degree, and taught there until 1908, when he went to Johns Hopkins, where behaviorism really began its existence as a separate school. He became involved in some personal problems at Hopkins in 1920, and, leaving his wife and academia, remarried and became an executive in a large New York advertising firm.

Watson proved himself as adept in his new career as he had been as a psychologist. Inventor of the early successful advertisement for Lucky Strike cigarettes, "Reach for a Lucky instead of a sweet" (incidentally, this advertising campaign, carefully engineered over several years, helped make it respectable for women to smoke), he was soon vice president of the company and made a very substantial, unacademic income. Retiring from advertising and psychology, he spent the last years of his life on a farm not far from New York City. During his advertising career, he published a few more books on behaviorism, based on his earlier thought; in 1957, one year before his death, the American Psychological Association honored him with a special award which pleased him tremendously, although his health was too poor to permit him to accept it in person. He had put his skills of persuasion to good use both in psychology and in the world of business.

### Watsonian Behaviorism

The first major statement of the behaviorist position was Watson's article in the 1913 *Psychological Review,* "Psychology as the Behaviorist Views It."[1]

[1] In the same year, in a paper in the *Journal of Philosophy,* Watson identified imagery with movements of the larynx, and feeling with glandular secretion, proposing behavioral substitutes for these previously purely subjective concepts.

In 1914 he published his *Behavior: An Introduction to Comparative Psychology.* This book and the *Psychological Review* article caused a major stir among American psychologists. His most systematic book, *Psychology from the Standpoint of a Behaviorist,* was published in 1919. Books on child psychology and on the development of personality, as well as some books for the popular trade, were published after this time.

Watson's *Behaviorism* (1925) contained the famous passage that showed how extremely environmentalistic his view was. Conditioning was the key to the understanding of behavior, and its potential was considered limitless. The rapid popularity of his position may at least in part be due to the fact that it fitted well with the American political ideology that all men are created equal and that anyone can achieve success. The passage is, "Give me a dozen healthy infants, well-formed, and my own specified world to bring them up in, and I'll guarantee to take any one at random and train him to become any type of specialist I might select—doctor, lawyer, artist, mer-chant-chief, and yes, begger-man and thief, regardless of his talents, tendencies, abilities, vocations, and the race of his ancestors." The later behaviorist B. F. Skinner, with his demonstration of the great power of reinforcement contingencies in shaping or molding behavior, might well have made a similar statement.

Watson's *Psychology from the Standpoint of a Behaviorist* had a very systematic outline. First it considered the problems and scope of psychology and psychological methods; then it followed the traditional, typical structuralist sequence, which behaviorism inherited from functionalism, and functionalism from structuralism: receptors and their stimuli, neurophysiological bases of action, the organs of response (muscles and glands), hereditary modes of response (instincts), emotions, the organism at work, personality, and abnormal behavior (the last three topics being included largely because of functionalism).

In his system, Watson argued that the subject matter of psychology is human and animal activity and conduct; psychology's aim is to predict behavior, to formulate laws about behavior, and to control behavior. Consciousness is not a legitimate subject for scientific study; only study of overt behavior is scientifically defensible. To be consistent, he went so far as to hold that thinking is verbal behavior; it consists of "subvocal speech," or minute movements of the vocal cords and tongue. The units of behavior are reflexes, or S-R connections, whether inborn or conditioned. Habits are overt or explicit (easily visible in behavior), or they are covert or implicit (more subtle internal processes); comparably, there are explicit hereditary reflexes and implicit hereditary reflexes. Although one can raise the question of whether implicit overt behavior may not be a self-contradictory concept, Watson argued that implicit behavior can often be measured, for example, by electrodes on the larynx during thinking or subvocal speech; furthermore, verbal report can be used as an index of implicit behavior. Fundamentally, all responses can be classified as glandular or muscular; ultimately, all we can do is secrete and contract.

The chief method of psychology is the study of the conditioned reflex, although other techniques for the observation of overt behavior, with or without the aid of instruments, are also appropriate. Thinking, as first suggested by Washburn and later developed by the behaviorists Max and Jacobson, can be studied by electrophysiological methods; the motor theory of thinking—that thinking is implicit movements—was enthusiastically defended on the ground that careful experimental work was indeed able occasionally to detect appropriate small muscle potentials during thought and during dreaming.[2]

Reflexes can, according to Watson, be classified into emotions, instincts, and habits; all are patterns of reflex arcs. The fundamental unit, the stimulus-response connection, or reflex arc, is combined with others and compounded into one of these three categories of behavior—a conception rather similar to James's notion of habit, and representing a version of the elementism so characteristic of early associationism as well as of later structuralism. Emotions involve the unstriped muscles, the instincts involve the striped. Emotions are internal activities, while instincts include the external situation; thus the emotions have a smaller scope than the instincts. Both are hereditary modes of action, sequences of chained reflex arcs, that unfold serially. Habits are learned modes of response, learned patterned concatenations, acquired arrangements of reflexes. The difference between a habit and an instinct, then, is that while both are complex sets of reflexes that function in a serial order, the instinct is inherited but the habit is acquired.

This systematic approach, with an emphasis upon the boundless explanatory power of conditioning, was applied by Watson to experimental and theoretical work on fear in childhood and to other aspects of developmental psychology, to child psychology, and to personality and abnormal psychology. Indeed, he was convinced that his system could handle all the problems of psychology, and handle them better than the prior—and contemporary— misguided subjective approaches. This, again, is a conviction that B. F. Skinner was later to hold about his own particular version of behaviorism, and to pass on enthusiastically to his followers.

---

[2] Here we have, incidentally, an example of uncritical belief in something, in the face of rather obviously fallacious reasoning, in the history of science: just because something like muscle potentials (A) is sometimes observed to go along with something like thought (B), this in no way demonstrates that A is identical to B, causes B, or even is a necessary concomitant of B. Partly because of this fallacy, nobody past the middle of the twentieth century took this kind of "motor theory of thinking" very seriously.

## LATER BEHAVIORISM

Although Watson was the chief systematizer and propagandist of behaviorism, there were others who made more important experimental contributions.

### Hunter

Walter S. Hunter (1889–1954), a student of Angell's and Carr's, spent many productive years at Brown University, and was one of the first to investigate the symbolic processes objectively. He concentrated upon the study of delayed reaction and of performance in the temporal maze. In the first, a stimulus indicating the correct response (such as a light over that one of a series of three doors which leads to a reward) is presented to the organism and then removed, and the organism is restrained from responding for some time, to see how long it can retain a memory of the stimulus, as demonstrated by a capacity still to be able to make the correct response, that is, to go to the correct door. The temporal maze was so constructed that either a right or a left turn eventually led back to the choice point, so that the only cue the organism had at the choice point was its memory of its preceding response; this device forced the animal to "count" the number of turns and also permitted the study of such things as patterns of alternation.

### Lashley

A major figure was Karl S. Lashley (1890–1958), whom we encountered briefly before; Lashley studied with Watson, and with Shepherd I. Franz (1874–1933), who trained Lashley in surgical techniques. As a result of his ablation studies, Lashley concluded in 1917 that learning is *not* a series of chained reflexes. He found that the amount of impairment in the performance of a learned habit is directly proportional to the amount of brain tissue removed—it did not seem to make much difference *what* part of the brain was cut out. It was this finding that led Lashley to his concepts of mass action, that the brain acts as a whole, and of equipotentiality, that different parts of the brain can take over similar functions.

### Hull and Tolman

Clark L. Hull (1884–1952) and Edward C. Tolman (1886–1959), both behaviorists—but very different kinds of behaviorists—were the learning theorists around whose formulations and controversies American psychology revolved in the 1940s and 1950s. Hull self-consciously employed a hypothetico-deductive method in his drive-reduction theory of learning. He formulated explicit postulates about learning, such as that reinforcement, in the sense of the reduction of a drive, is essential for any learning to occur, and deduced theorems from these postulates, then tested the validity of his theory by experimental studies in the laboratory, mostly with rats. His influence on the field of learning was very great, and he acquired many avid followers. Tolman, not as systematic as Hull, was less concerned with the hooking up of stimuli and responses than with more molar response patterns and the learning of what he called "sign-gestalt-expectations," by which he meant, roughly, what is a sign for what, or what leads to what. He disagreed with Hull on the necessity for drive-reducing reinforcement in learning, and felt that what is learned is the characteristics of the environment, the consequences of various actions, and the like. His was a more cognitive form of behaviorism.

### Guthrie and Skinner

Edwin R. Guthrie (1886–1959), professor and later Graduate Dean at the University of Washington, proposed a theory of behavior based upon a single law: any time a response occurs, it is linked forever with each of the stimulus elements present at the time the response is made. Widely influential, this formulation was later used as part of the assumptions of some elementary early mathematical models of learning. Guthrie also showed how it could be used in the analysis of social phenomena and personality, and be applied in educational psychology. He based his theory in part upon an extensive experiment on cats in a puzzle box, patterned after the work of Thorndike, and performed some ten years before Guthrie by Karl F. Muenzinger at Colorado. Muenzinger too published a highly systematic small volume, *Psychology: The Science of Behavior,* in 1939.

B. F. Skinner (1904–    ), to whom we have often alluded before, proved to be the most objective, and, in the second half of the twentieth century, by far the most influential behaviorist of them all; he was unwilling to admit any concept of implicit behavior, or even any hypothetical constructs. Using a strictly operationalized definition of reinforcement (anything is a reinforcer if it increases the probability of a preceding response), he produced a very powerful, pure, descriptive behaviorism, and amassed a very wide and enthusiastic following. His approach has had a profound impact, among other areas, on teaching machines and programmed learning.

### Other Post-Watsonian Developments

Fundamentally, there are two kinds of behaviorists: the molecular, concerned with muscular reactions as Watson, Hull, Spence, and Guthrie, and the more molar, concerned with larger purposive reactions, as

McDougall, Tolman, and to some extent Lashley. For the molecular behaviorist, the prime unit is the reflex or the S-R connection, an atomistic, elementistic conception; for the molar behaviorist the fundamental unit is the molar act. The molecularists generally have inclined toward a reinforcement view, while the molar behaviorists have tended more to favor a cognitive map view—in other words, that behavior is determined by how the organism cognizes its field. Skinner in a way bridged the gap, being interested in the contingencies relating acts and consequences (or reinforcements) in specific settings. Behaviorists generally have been concerned with the use of behavior, much as the functionalists were; most behaviorists, both molecular and molar, have been associationistic and mechanistic in their psychological and neurological concepts.

The physicalistic elementaristic trend in modern learning psychology is only one of several developments that grew out of Watsonian behaviorism. That trend had developed from his concern with habit; later workers also further developed his doctrines of emotion and of instinct. Max Meyer began a tradition in American psychology of banishing emotions as inappropriate to objective study; during the 1930s and 1940s hardly any self-respecting psychologist permitted himself to use the term. The same happened with the concept of instinct, which Knight Dunlap (1875–1949) attacked.[3]

Interest in instinctive behavior, however, came back into fashion in the late 1940s and 1950s. Leaders among the ethologists—biologists studying animal behavior, typically in the natural habitat—were Konrad Lorenz and Nikolaas Tinbergen, who undertook ingenious studies of the complex behavior patterns of lower organisms. They investigated the stimuli and situations that trigger these patterns, as well as certain critical age periods in the learning or imprinting of certain complex behaviors such as a duckling's following of its mother.

## THE IMPACT OF BEHAVIORISM

The fundamental tenet of all behaviorism is strict objectivity: one must study overt behavior and leave out consciousness. The use of objective observation rather than some version of introspection as the method of preference became very widespread by the middle of the twentieth century

---

[3] According to both Dunlap's and Watson's chapters in *A History of Psychology in Autobiography,* Dunlap claimed that he himself formulated the principles of behaviorism and that Watson got them from him. The chapters indicate further that Watson recognized that he did get the systematic structure for behaviorism from Dunlap. This bit of information, which came to the present writer from Julian Jaynes of Princeton via E. G. Boring of Harvard after the manuscript for this book was completed, suggests that Knight Dunlap should receive more space and more credit in future discussions of the history of behaviorism.

among U.S. psychologists; the vast majority tended in this direction, and in this sense modern American psychology became behavioristic.

The behaviorism of the early part of the latter half of the twentieth century could perhaps be characterized as a kind of physicalism, in part influenced by the logical positivist movement in philosophy, which in turn arose out of the critical empiricist tradition. It is now widely held that the description of psychological data should be in "cgs terms"—that is, one must make measurements in units like centimeters, grams, and seconds; only in this way can psychology be a true science. The need to objectify the phenomena one is studying came to be accepted by almost all modern psychologists, whether or not they considered themselves behaviorists or operationists or physicalists or logical positivists.

# 13

# Gestalt
# Psychology

## ANTECEDENTS OF GESTALT PSYCHOLOGY

The German word *Gestalt* itself is hard to translate; Titchener suggested the term configuration, but somehow this did not catch on. Possible other translations are form, or pattern, or structure, all of which give some impression of the meaning of the word, but none of which alone exactly captures the meaning of the German term; so the word *gestalt* has become part of the technical vocabulary of psychology. Long before the formal development of the gestalt school in psychology and philosophy, Goethe had used the term and concept in a manner that to some degree anticipated its later use by the gestalt psychologists.

There were also other anticipations and antecedents of gestalt psychology, as we have pointed out repeatedly in previous chapters. Although they were not direct anticipators, John Stuart Mill, with his idea of mental chemistry, put forth a similar notion; William James emphasized that the stream of consciousness is a whole, a totality; John Dewey's criticism of the reflex arc concept was wholistic; and even Wilhelm Wundt had emphasized the process of creative synthesis. The philosopher-physicist Ernst Mach used phenomenology much in the way the later gestalt psychologists did.

### Ehrenfels and Gestaltqualität

The Austrian university at Graz became the center of the Gestaltqualität school, mostly in the person of Christian von Ehrenfels (1859–1932), but leavened also by the leader of the "Graz school," Alexius Meinong

(1853–1920). In 1890 Ehrenfels published a paper in which he insisted that Wundt's psychology had neglected a very important element: the form quality, or Gestaltqualität.

Form quality, for Ehrenfels, is an element over and above the elements composing a whole. A melody played in a given key is not just the sum of the notes, but is, in addition, their total configuration. Change the relations among the elements, and the whole changes. But you can transpose the melody, that is, put it into a different key and thus change all the elements, yet still retain the melody itself, the Gestaltqualität, as long as the *relations* among the individual elements or notes remain the same. Dependence upon relations among elements and transposability are the essential properties of form qualities. Thus form qualities include, in addition to melodies, such properties as triangularity, roundness, squareness. The emphasis upon transposition was also to emerge later in the form of transposition experiments with children and animals; subjects tend to respond not so much to absolute brightness or size as to relations like relative brightness, being the largest item in a set, and so forth. Learned relationships among objects can be transposed to new sets of objects.

### Phenomenology

The phenomenological method was basic to gestalt psychology. Among the predecessors of the gestaltists was Stumpf, who influenced all three of the leading early gestalt psychologists, Wertheimer, Koffka, and Köhler. David Katz (1884–1953), a student of G. E. Müller at Göttingen, undertook a detailed phenomenology of color perception. Edgar Rubin (1886–1951), another student of Müller's, wrote his Ph.D. dissertation on the distinction between figure and ground, which was later to be picked up by the gestalt psychologists (although the study itself was performed several years after the gestalt movement had become firmly established). Harry Helson (1889–    ), who obtained his Ph.D. with Boring at Harvard, examined the antecedent and contemporaneous gestalt trends in great detail; this work, as was mentioned before, was published as a series of articles and as a monograph by the *American Journal of Psychology* in 1925 and 1926.

### THE FOUNDERS OF GESTALT PSYCHOLOGY

The founders of the gestalt school were Max Wertheimer, Kurt Koffka, and Wolfgang Köhler. Wertheimer made the original statement, and the other two later accepted and elaborated it. A fourth important gestalt psychologist, somewhat younger than the other three, was Kurt Lewin. All emphasized the principle of relational determination—that is, that properties of parts depend upon the relation of the parts to the whole; part qualities depend upon the place, role, and function of the part in the whole. They also held that in most configurations the whole does not equal the sum of its parts. Central to their thinking was Wertheimer's law of prägnanz, which stated that the organization of any whole is as good as the prevailing conditions allow.

### Wertheimer

Max Wertheimer (1880–1943) obtained his Ph.D. summa cum laude under Külpe in 1904, after having vacillated among careers in music, philosophy, and psychology. He was at the University of Frankfurt in 1910, went to the University of Berlin in 1916, and in 1933 came to the United States, where he taught at the New School for Social Research in New York until his death ten years later. A deep thinker, a gentle, warm man with a walrus moustache, he was a close friend of the physicist Albert Einstein.

In 1910 Wertheimer realized the major systematic significance of the fact that discontinuous visual stimulation can yield the perception of continuous movement—the percept, it appears, does not correspond point-for-point with the physical stimulus, but is organized as a whole—a whole which is not just the sum-total of the elements composing it. The paper in which this material was presented, on experimental studies in the perception of movement, was published in 1912.[1] In the same year there appeared a paper on the thinking of primitive peoples, in which he argued that thought is not associationistic, but configural, and "makes sense." Other early publications were also on the psychology of thought.

In 1923 Wertheimer published a very influential paper on the organization of perception, arguing for a nonempiristic view of how percepts arise out of the punctiform activity of neural elements on the receptor surface. Those parts of the perceptual field are organized together, are perceived as belonging together or as forming a unit, which are similar and close to each other, which move together or constitute a "good" form. In 1925 three of the early fundamental papers were published together in book form; another brief paper on gestalt psychology, summarizing the work up to that date, was published in the same year.

[1] The story goes that Wertheimer was on the train from Vienna for a vacation on the Rhine when he got the idea of the relation of phenomenal movement to a full-blown gestalt orientation to all of psychology. He was so excited that he got off the train at Frankfurt, where he had not intended to get off. He went to a toy store and bought a little stroboscope and began tinkering with it in his hotel room. He called on Friedrich Schumann at the University of Frankfurt, was shown the newly constructed Schumann tachistoscope, was invited to stay, and went to work. Köhler and Koffka thereafter went to Frankfurt from Berlin and stayed there until the work required for the 1912 paper was finished, serving mostly as subjects. According to Koffka (via Boring), he and Köhler did not realize the significance of Wertheimer's work until it was done, when Wertheimer told Köhler and then later Koffka.

Later writings showed the breadth of applicability of gestalt principles, with analyses of philosophical issues such as ethics, truth, and the concept of democracy. *Productive Thinking,* a small volume which presented in detail the gestalt approach to thinking and problem solving, was published posthumously. A problem exists when something is not clear, does not fit together, has a gap; this disturbance produces a striving to resolve the lack of clarity, and the solution results in everything fitting together and making sense.

### Koffka

Kurt Koffka (1886–1941) obtained his Ph.D. from Stumpf, then taught at the University in Giessen in central Germany. In 1922 he published the first article in English on gestalt psychology, in the *Psychological Bulletin;* its title, which was to begin a long tradition of misunderstanding of the significance of perception in gestalt psychology, was "Perception: An Introduction to the *Gestalt-Theorie.*" (Gestalt theory was primarily concerned with thinking, with philosophical questions, and with learning; the main reason why the early gestalt psychologists concentrated their systematic publications on perception was because of the Zeitgeist: Wundt's psychology, against which the gestaltists rebelled, had obtained most of its support from studies of sensation and perception, so the gestalt psychologists chose perception as the arena in order to attack Wundt in his own stronghold— sensory and perceptual processes.) The paper elaborated especially on the central thesis that the "constancy hypothesis" (that is, that the relationship between local stimulus and percept is constant) is untenable, citing many experimental findings to support this attack against structuralism and providing a solid experimental base for the principles of the new school.

In 1924 Koffka accepted a research professorship at Smith College in the United States, where he stayed until his death. Together with Wertheimer and Köhler, he founded the journal *Psychologische Forschung,* the primary outlet for the research of the gestalt psychologists in the 1920s and 1930s. In 1921 he published a book on child psychology, later translated as *The Growth of the Mind.* The only fully systematic major gestalt psychological treatise, *Principles of Gestalt Psychology,* was published by Koffka in 1936.

### Köhler

Wolfgang Köhler (1887–1967), like Koffka, obtained his Ph.D. from Stumpf at Berlin; he remained there for several years after his degree. He and Koffka came to the University of Frankfurt at the time Wertheimer was beginning his experiments on the perception of movement; both he and Koffka served as subjects for these experiments.

In 1914 Köhler was marooned by the First World War at Tenerife, one of the Canary Islands, where the Prussian Academy of Science maintained an anthropoid station. He remained on the island, working with the chimpanzee colony, through the entire war. Thereafter he returned to the University of Berlin, and published in 1917 the German version of the book later translated into English as *The Mentality of Apes;* the original German title of the book is more adequately translated as *Intelligence Tests with Anthropoid Apes.* This highly readable volume was based on a series of lectures about his experiments on Tenerife. The experiments showed the importance of insight and understanding in problem solving.

In 1920 Köhler published a difficult but significant book, which has unfortunately never been translated into English: *The Physical Gestalten at Rest and in a Stationary State,* in which he described physical gestalten in chemistry, electricity, and biology, and argued that the gestalt fields which occur in physical phenomena should also occur in brain processes. His work of later years elaborated further on this doctrine of isomorphism, first presented in Wertheimer's 1912 paper on movement; specifically, isomorphism holds that psychological phenomena and the brain processes underlying the psychological phenomena have a similar functional form, show similar gestalt properties. Here, finally, was a physiological alternative to the neural hookups that had dominated thought in physiological psychology for centuries.

In 1934 Köhler came to the United States after having written a daring letter to a newspaper against naziism; the prestige of a Berlin professorship was insufficient, so he had to escape. He lectured at Harvard, then went to Swarthmore College in 1935, and stayed there for many years in spite of a number of efforts to entice him elsewhere. Among his other books were *Gestalt Psychology* in 1929, *The Place of Value in a World of Facts* in 1938, and *Dynamics in Psychology* in 1940—all systematic developments of the gestalt position. In the 1940s and 1950s he published extensive experimental work on figural aftereffects, a class of perceptual illusions which was implied directly by his isomorphic theory.

Köhler loved New England, and spent many summers on Mt. Desert Island, off the coast of Maine. On his retirement he made Dartmouth College his headquarters, and continued his research and writing; after retiring from Swarthmore he also spent several semesters teaching at European universities, both in Scandinavia and on the Continent.[2]

---

[2] A fastidious, meticulous man with the highest personal standards, Köhler loved to be immaculate in everything he did. The present writer has fond memories from the 1940s of seeing Köhler, bent on recreation, spending a Sunday afternoon chopping firewood in his back yard—using a razor-sharp, well-polished axe, and dressed in a spotless white suit, with white shirt and tie.

## THE TENETS OF GESTALT PSYCHOLOGY

The gestalt movement itself began in 1910 when Wertheimer conceived his stroboscopic motion experiment and   performed it on his two subjects, Köhler and Koffka. Ehrenfels had said that the whole is more than the sum of its parts; the gestalt psychologists went beyond this and held that the whole is different from the sum of its parts. The whole-quality is not just one more added element. Wertheimer's insight was that what happens in the experiment on stroboscopic movement is typical of almost all experience and behavior; indeed that gestalt principles hold in virtually every field of philosophy, art, and science. The qualities of the whole determine the characteristics of the parts; what a part has to be is determined by its place, role, and function in the whole of which it is a part. The "law of prägnanz" holds that the organization of any whole will be as good as the prevailing conditions allow.

Bare associations are rare limiting cases of psychological processes. To be sure, we do associate such things as telephone numbers and people, but this kind of association is atypical. What usually happens, argued the gestaltists, is a much more dynamic unfolding of events such that the nature of the things connected is at least in part affected by the connection and in turn affects the connection. Most psychological processes and events are not senseless agglutinations ("sinnlose Und-Verbindungen") or hookups ("Kuppelungen") which come about through blind connections as between phone numbers and people's names. Most acts are "organized from the inside," as it were; they make sense, are meaningful.

This formulation involved a radical reorientation: the nature of the parts is determined by the whole rather than vice versa; therefore analysis should go "from above down" rather than "from below up." One should not begin with elements and try to synthesize the whole from them, but study the whole to see what its natural parts are. The parts of a whole are not neutral and inert, but structurally intimately related to one another. That parts of a whole are not indifferent to one another was illustrated, for example, by a soap bubble: change of one part results in a dramatic change in the entire configuration. This approach was applied to the concrete understanding of a wide variety of phenomena in thinking, learning, problem solving, perception, and philosophy, and the movement developed and spread rapidly, with violent criticisms against it from outside, as well as equally vehement attacks on the outsiders from inside.

The militancy of the position, and what it was militant about, can be seen in some of the arguments in Köhler's *Gestalt Psychology*. Köhler held that the "orthodox" viewpoints in psychology, as he called introspectionism (that is, structuralism) and behaviorism, are wrong in assuming "and-conections" in behavior and in the brain. Relations among parts are conditioned by the properties of the parts, and are not empty hookups or stringlike connections such as are implied by use of the words "plus" or "and." Field processes are widespread.

Köhler provides examples from physics: the planetary system depends upon certain self-distributing gravitational forces in dynamic relation. The forces of steam are similarly not machinelike; they have more than one degree of freedom. True, they can be channeled into man-made, prearranged pipes or pathways, as in a steam engine; but in its natural state the force of steam is not restricted to a single direction. If one places a drop of oil or mercury in water it becomes a sphere by its own dynamic properties, not by any mold into which it is poured; the dynamic self-distribution of forces results in the spherical form of the globule: these forces come from within.

Such an orientation is in sharp contrast to the machine model which was at least implicit in associationism, structuralism, functionalism, behaviorism; the dynamic model of the gestaltists argues that physical forces, when released, do not produce chaos, but their own internally determined organization. The nervous system, similarly, is not characterized by ma-chinelike connections of tubes, grooves, wires, or switchboards, but the brain too, like almost all other physical systems, exhibits the dynamic self-distribution of physical forces. Köhler argued that the observed mind-body parallelism requires that such self-determination also display itself in experience and behavior.

The contrast of dynamic self-distribution with machine theory is, incidentally, also evident in the contrast between the ancient Aristotelian notion of crystal spheres which hold the planets and the stars in place and the later less machinelike notions of post-Renaissance astronomers. The machine theory explanation of the order of the universe, with all its fanciful, artificial mechanical restraints, gave way to the modern one based on inertia, gravitation, .and revolution, an explanation in terms of dynamic self-distribution; the field of forces, rather than some mechanical crystal spheres, holds the planets in their orbits. The similarity between Einstein's field formulations in physics and some of the gestalt ideas, incidentally, is no accident, but can be traced in part to many long conversations between Einstein and Wertheimer, especially during the first two decades of the twentieth century.

Köhler also contrasted the Jamesian and Watsonian notion of concatena-tions of reflexes with his gestalt explanation of his chimpanzees' behavior during problem solving; the dynamic explanation, which Köhler espoused, used the concept of insight. It is not blind trial and error or rewarded S-R connections which explain the behavior; rather, the animal understands the structure of the problem situation, and acts accordingly. The main point he made so successfully and so forcefully is that it is possible to achieve an understanding of the genesis of order rather than chaos, not only through the constraint of machine ideas, but also via the free play of orderly forces—that is, via dynamic self-distribution—without necessarily being "vitalistic." It was his genius to draw convincing demonstrations from soap films, electrical fields, and the like, as well as from psychological phenomena.

## LEWIN AND LATER GESTALT PSYCHOLOGY

While the founders of gestalt psychology had concentrated on cognitive processes such as learning, thinking, intelligence, and perception, Kurt Lewin (1890–1947) concerned himself mostly with applying the principles of dynamic self-distribution of forces, the restructuring of the field, and insight, to motivation, personality, and social processes. His later work on small groups, from which the rapidly spreading field of group dynamics (the empirical study of interaction within groups, and of group productivity as a function of group structure) arose, and his analysis of child behavior, made ingenious use of the dynamic gestalt principles, which some later writers rechristened "field theory," in line with Köhler's earlier use of the term to characterize the gestalt approach. Lewin tried to understand the person and his situation as the person himself sees it, in terms of his life space, with its various psychological barriers and valences, the person's likes and dislikes of objects, people, activities. He put these concepts, together with tensions (such as that produced by an unresolved problem) and vectors (such as a motive or tendency to see a movie or go to a concert), into topological symbols, with the hope of being better able to manipulate them in this form.

Considered a friendly, outgoing, and warm person by almost everyone who came in contact with him, Lewin obtained his Ph.D. at the University of Berlin, then served in the First World War, and returned to Berlin as the equivalent of an assistant professor. He came to the United States several times, and in 1933 decided to stay; after some minor appointments, including one at Cornell University, he was made full professor at the University of Iowa, where he worked primarily in child and in social psychology. In 1945, having become renowned through his work on small groups, he was asked to head a new Research Center for Group Dynamics at the Massachusetts Institute of Technology. He went there with a group of students, and it was at MIT that the school of group dynamics flourished, although he was to live only two more years. Lewin had strong disciples, who carried on his approach after Lewin's death, primarily at MIT, at the University of Kansas, and at the University of Michigan. The group dynamics work soon was known throughout all of the United States. Lewin published a number of influential books, including *Dynamic Theory of Personality,* and several on his topological and vector psychology; he also contributed chapters to a number of handbooks.

The influence of Lewin spread rapidly, and many psychologists, especially American ones, were much indebted to him and his teachings. But the more traditional gestalt approach also had its later adherents. Thus there was Hans Wallach, who devoted most of his work to perception, and Solomon Asch, who developed in detail Wertheimer's insights into the social psychological implications of a gestalt orientation. Kurt Goldstein's work in neurology played a major role in the early development of gestalt theory, and his organismic and personality theory were much influenced by gestalt principles; with Martin Scheerer he also studied thinking disorders in people with brain injuries, using a gestalt approach. Abraham Maslow, too, developed a gestalt-oriented theory of self-actualization, and applied the approach to motivation and personality in a somewhat different way than Goldstein or Lewin. Abraham Luchins, a jack-of-all-trades gestalt psychologist, began his career with widely cited studies under Wertheimer of the effect of set on problem solving, and branched out into clinical and social psychology, as well as continuing his interest in more classical areas. Rudolf Arnheim developed the implications of gestalt theory for esthetics. We have already had occasion several times, too, to refer to the influence of gestalt thinking on Edward Tolman's approach to learning. In Europe, centers of research on perception which were greatly affected by the gestalt approach flourished under L. Kardos at Budapest, Wolfgang Metzger at Münster, Kai von Fieandt at Helsinki, and Albert Michotte at Louvain, among others.

## THE IMPACT OF GESTALT PSYCHOLOGY

When gestalt psychology came to the United States, it was generally received with great interest, sometimes with politeness, and sometimes with suspicion; it has been conjectured that the American attitude toward gestalt psychology was tinged with the same xenophobia that was hinted at in the United States reception of people like Titchener, McDougall, and Münsterberg. The attitude toward Freud doubtless also partook of this suspicion of foreigners. Koffka, Wertheimer, and Lewin were never fully accepted by organized American psychology, but Köhler was; in his late years, he received the American Psychological Association's Distinguished Scientific Contribution Award, and won the honor and recognition of being elected president of the American Psychological Association in 1958.

The gestalt movement played a significant role in the revolt against structuralism. Its objections to elementism went beyond its critique of structuralism, however, and were applied to S-R behaviorism as well. Gestalt psychology called attention to the usefulness of field concepts and to various problems which might otherwise have been ignored, such as insight in animals and humans, the organized nature of perception, of experience, the richness of genuine thought processes, and in general to the utility of dealing in larger, molar, organized units, taking full account of their nature and structure. One should not analyze arbitrarily into predetermined elements, since such analysis, the gestaltists argued, and most psychologists now recognize, may do violence to the intrinsic meaning of the whole.

Although the gestalt school no longer existed as a major movement after the middle of the twentieth century, the issues it raised, and raised successfully, in opposition to the prevalent oversimplified S-R, mechanistic, hookup psychology typical especially of American associationistic behaviorism, continued to be central in psychological thought. The gestalt school had done its job well, leaving a lasting mark on the discipline, in the psychology of cognition, perception, thinking, and learning, and in motivation, personality, and social psychology—indeed in almost all fields.

# 14

# Psychoanalysis

## ANTECEDENTS OF PSYCHOANALYSIS

The psychoanalytic movement was not really part of the same set of developments that led to the other schools; among other things, it focused primarily on abnormal behavior and what to do about it and hence asked quite different questions than the other schools did. Its historical beginnings must be sought elsewhere. Although it was influenced by Darwin's concept of evolution, it had no real roots in physiology; it was only distantly, if at all, atomistic and had little to do with laboratories, scientific materialism, or with the quantitative approach. There was perhaps a minor hint of associationism, and only a dim relation to critical empiricism. Rather, one might relate psychoanalysis more to the romantic tradition and to the history of medical and clinical psychology, which we have hardly touched on at all. The work on hypnotic phenomena by such men as Mesmer, Esdaile, Braid, and later Liébeault and Charcot had a direct influence upon Freud's thinking.

Then there is the long history of concern with the mentally ill. An early highlight is the *Malleus Maleficarum,* or "hammer for witches" (an excellent descriptive psychiatry written in the Middle Ages by two monks). One must also mention Philippe Pinel, who pleaded late in the eighteenth century that people suffering from mental illness are not possessed by demons, are not incurable, and should not be morally censured, but are sick and need help. We have already referred to Kraepelin's careful classification of the mental disorders late in the nineteenth century. These people and the ideas they developed would require a whole book to themselves in order to treat them thoroughly.

Since almost everybody is familiar with Freud and psychoanalysis, and since many excellent secondary sources are available—as well as the fact that psychoanalysis is largely unrelated to traditional experimental psychology—we will do no more here than touch very briefly on some of the more central concepts in psychoanalytic theory. It is an entirely different way of thinking than what usually goes by the name of psychology, and is a vastly complex specialty.

## FREUDIAN PSYCHOANALYSIS

Psychoanalysis consists of a theory of personality, a philosophy of the nature of man, and a procedure for psychotherapy. The intellectual giant who developed this approach was Sigmund Freud (1856–1939). Basing his approach on the conception of an active unconscious mind of the kind hinted at by Shakespeare, Goethe, Brentano, Fechner, and Herbart, Freud went far beyond his predecessors.

### Freud

Freud spent most of his life in Vienna; he initiated his medical career with work in neurology, but soon devoted himself exclusively to psychopathology and personality. Early in his career he worked with Joseph Breuer (1842–1925) in the application of hypnotic techniques to the treatment of hysteria, following the ideas of Pierre Janet (1859–1947); then he studied hypnosis with Jean-Martin Charcot (1825–1893) at Paris for a while. It was Charcot, it seems, who first planted in Freud's mind the idea that sexual problems play the decisive role in the etiology of neurotic disorders.

After his sojourn in Paris, Freud returned to his practice with Breuer, and together they gradually worked out the therapeutic technique of free association, in which the patient is required to talk without any censorship about anything and everything that comes into his mind. Breuer soon felt uncomfortable about the strong attachment ("transference") patients developed for the therapist with this new technique, and about Freud's growing conviction concerning the importance of sexuality, so Freud continued on his way alone.

Freud further developed the method of free association, and began to make use of dream interpretation; a major early book, *The Interpretation of Dreams*, was published in 1900. He published many other influential works, and his theory continued, ever changing, to evolve until his death in 1939. Gradually, from the turn of the century on, Freud's ideas attracted first a small, and then a continuously wider group of devoted followers, and by the second decade of the twentieth century the psychoanalytic movement was broadly international in scope.

### Freud's Theories

The appeal of the movement was primarily to medically trained psychiatrists, although psychoanalysis also soon developed a wide popular following. Indeed, even to the day of the present writing, many laymen tend to equate psychology and psychoanalysis. But psychology as an academic discipline, as we have indicated, has been relatively little influenced by Freudian thought —except that much practice and theory in clinical psychology by the middle of the twentieth century had become quite Freudian.

The lack of interest in psychoanalysis on the part of traditional academic psychology may at least be partly traced to the fact that Freud and his followers attacked a different kind of problem than that which had been sanctioned as psychology by Wundt and the early experimental psychologists. It is also interesting to speculate that possibly one contributory reason why American psychology of the first decades of the twentieth century all but ignored psychoanalysis may be nothing but an accidental mistranslation: Freud's core concept of *Trieb* was rendered into English as "instinct" rather than "drive," with which the German word is actually linguistically related, and whose English meaning is closer to Freud's use of "Trieb" than "instinct" is; the American Ortgeist was decidedly anti-instinct during the first half of the twentieth century.

As we have indicated, Freud's views continued to evolve during his long and fruitful career. Nevertheless, let us select a few of the more important concepts and principles he proposed, in order to provide a brief review of the nature and flavor of psychoanalytic thought.

Freud taught that every act, every thought, is motivated; the fundamental human moving force is the libido, a violently selfish, aggressive sexual drive which constitutes the id, literally the "it," of the personality. Everyone has in himself a creative, sexual force (eros) and a destructive, aggressive push toward death (thanatos). Early in life the infant discovers that having a drive does not necessarily lead to its satisfaction; one must somehow come to terms with the world, and manipulate it in such a way as to satisfy one's desires. This leads to the growth of the ego, which mediates between the pleasure principle of the id and the reality principle which dominates interactions with the environment. The child's parents attempt the almost hopeless task of socializing the id, trying to tame the selfish impulses that constitute the infant's inborn drives; this leads to the development of a superego, a kind of conscience, which makes the person feel guilty any time an id impulse is permitted to express itself.

The ego is charged with the difficult task of trying to make peace between the id, which says, "I want," and the superego, which says, "I shouldn't," as well as having to mediate between both of these and the relentlessly realistic outside world. In trying to do so, the ego sees to it that the id remains totally unconscious, the superego remains almost entirely so, and even the ego itself is only in part conscious. The ego is forced to employ complex and ingenious techniques for keeping unacceptable impulses from rising into consciousness, using defense mechanisms such as repression, sublimation, and other forms of distortion and self-deception. The Oedipus complex, or the unconscious desire for the death of the parent of the same sex and for physical union with the parent of the opposite sex, is among the quandaries which the ego must somehow try to handle.

The task of the ego, according to Freud, is made more difficult because early in the individual's development the primary focus of the libidinal drive moves from one part of the body to another. Characterized as polymorphous perverse infantile sexuality, libidinal satisfaction is first obtained primarily through the oral zone, with the pleasure that the infant derives from feeding. With toilet training, the anal region becomes the primary erogenous zone; next there is the phallic stage, followed, after a latent period in which sexuality is totally repressed, by maturity or the genital stage, in which libidinal gratification is obtained through adult heterosexual union. The individual may become fixated at any of these psychosexual stages, and even the mature, reasonably well-adjusted adult typically is considered to have some immature vestiges of his earlier psychosexual development. It was one of Freud's most influential teachings that there is a continuum from normal to abnormal, that the two are not qualitatively different.

### Freudian Psychotherapy

The process of psychoanalysis, or of trying to uncover the unconscious, irrational determinants of behavior, which are usually to be found in emotionally tinged childhood experiences, involves primarily free association and dream analysis. In free association, the patient reports whatever comes to his mind, attempting to circumvent the ego's censor. Dreams are, according to Freud, "the royal road to the unconscious"; in them, symbolic material providing hints about unconscious processes is much easier for both analyst and analysand to discover, particularly if the patient free associates to the important elements of the dream. Psychoanalysis maintains that knowing the truth about himself will set the patient free; to the extent that he becomes aware of the forces in his unconscious, the patient becomes less their unwitting prisoner, and can lead a more rational, satisfying, and productive life.

## JUNG, ADLER, AND LATER PSYCHOANALYSTS

Two major early offshoots of Freudian psychoanalysis were the analytical psychology of Carl Gustav Jung (1875–1961) and the individual psychology of Alfred Adler (1870–1937). The analytical psychology of Jung, with his concept of the archetypes (fundamental modes of experience, like that of religious awe, the sense of evil, and so forth), his emphasis upon introversion and extraversion, and his mental functions of thinking, feeling, sensing, and intuiting, was based on a rich ground of scholarly knowledge of comparative symbolism and mythology and of extensive, sensitive clinical practice. Jung's is a highly intricate system, placing less emphasis upon sex than has Freud's, but fully as complex, if not more so, in its ingenious ramifications.

Adler's individual psychology, with a smaller number of quite powerful concepts and principles, is somewhat simpler than either Freud's or Jung's theories. The young child is inevitably weak in comparison with adults, and this has the effect that throughout the remainder of his life everyone strives to overcome the inferiority feelings engendered by these early experiences. The will to power is produced in everyone, as an attempt to compensate for early inferiority. Ultimately every individual develops his own particular style of life for overcoming inferiority and handling the problems of interpersonal interaction. At its best, the style of life is, according to Adler, a creative, positive approach permitting the individual to devote his energies to constructive pursuits.

There were other important later figures in psychoanalysis. Otto Rank (1884–1939) tried to understand man's problems in terms of the trauma of birth, and emphasized man's creative nature. Sandor Ferenczi (1873–1933) attributed many neurotic problems to the need for mother love. Karen Horney (1885–1952), Erich Fromm (1900–     ) and Harry Stack Sullivan (1892–1949), all pointed to the interpersonal and social origins of neurotic conflicts, and were influential in the development of what has been called neo-Freudian psychoanalysis. A major emphasis of the neo-Freudians has been ego function, with a relative decline of interest in intrapersonal id processes. For many of them, the aim of psychoanalytic work is to provide the patient with an ego strong enough to assist him in coping with the inevitably anxiety-producing problems inherent in interpersonal interactions, and to make it possible for him to make full productive use of his particular, unique human endowments.

# 15

# The

# Postschools Era

## AN OVERVIEW

As psychology, especially American psychology, entered the last third of the twentieth century, it had become a huge, self-respecting, diverse endeavor, almost unrecognizably different from its counterpart a century earlier. Yet in many respects the assumptions and methods of the later psychologist were not so different from those of his earlier colleague. The eight trends we reviewed in Part I were still discernible.

As for the scientific trends, many psychologists, from comparative psychologists through psychoneurobiochemists to behavioral geneticists, were working on *biological* and *physiological* correlates of behavior. *Atomism* remained there, among other places, in factor analysis, in the study of the single cell, the conditional response, and the behavior of the computer. Sophistication in *quantitative* methods, in statistical techniques and in complex mathematical models, had grown at a fantastic rate. *Laboratories* and institutes were being *founded* right and left, by colleges, universities, foundations, and government agencies.

The philosophical trends were clearly still there too. *Associationism* flourished in learning theory, in the field of verbal behavior, and in most approaches to perceptual learning. *Critical empiricism* was everywhere, with constantly more refined and sophisticated methods and techniques for obtaining nice, clean, uncontaminated data about every aspect of behavior one could imagine. And finally, many psychologists were vigorously pursuing *scientific materialism,* that is, were thinking in terms of an "empty organism," or of "neuromythology," the C.N.S. or conceptual nervous system, of real or fanciful underlying physiological processes; scientific materialism remained very much alive.

The characteristics of the postschools era in psychology suggest that psychology was leaving its stormy adolescence and entering upon maturity. There was less of the militant insistence that psychology is a science; there was less rebellion against psychology's parent, philosophy; there was less interschool derision. A major trend was the quiet but powerful onslaught of objective empirical method, entering upon complex terrain that had never before been studied scientifically. This trend was greatly strengthened by the vast sums of money which foundations and government agencies made available for behavioral research—indeed, behavioral science had become big business, and one could call the middle of the twentieth century the age of sponsored research. Much of this work cut across traditional disciplinary boundaries; psychologists collaborated with physiologists, mathematicians, anthropologists, sociologists, physicists, psychiatrists, engineers—perhaps, then, one could also call this the era of interdisciplinary research.

Aside from the growing diversity of areas studied empirically, which was perhaps the most significant recent trend, two other major developments were the spread of professionalism in psychology and the growing importance of mathematics in psychology. A very substantial fraction of American psychologists were clinical psychologists, but there were many other people engaged in the practice of psychology: there were industrial psychologists, advertising men, human engineers, pollsters, military psychologists, management consultants, and still others. Psychology had fully achieved professional status as well as being an academic discipline. And the trend toward quantification, which grew gradually during the eighteenth and nineteenth centuries, received a major impetus with the advent of the high-speed electronic computer: what previously had been prohibitively tedious, lengthy, and complex computations were reduced to ready feasibility.

Let us briefly examine each of these three trends—the development of new empirical approaches, the service aspects of psychology, and quantification—in turn. But first, we shall consider the logical positivist movement and operationism, for particularly the second of these has played, at least implicitly, a major role in the growing power of empirical method in psychology.

## OPERATIONISM

Logical positivism was a philosophical movement started in Vienna during the second decade of the twentieth century; one of its godfathers was Ernst Mach. An outgrowth of critical empiricism, it concerned itself with trying to determine what it is that one can be sure about, or, in other words, what information can be used for the founding of an epistemology. In a sense it was a kind of negativism, in that the older logical positivist position denied the reality of phenomena that are not directly observable; it tried hard to avoid falling into an examination of "pseudo-problems," which no information could possibly resolve.

Related to logical positivism is the operationism of Percy Bridgman (1882–1961), a physicist, who held that the meaning of any concept is the set of operations required to demonstrate that concept. It was primarily S. S. Stevens (1906–    ) who developed operationism in psychology; just as is true of any other scientific concept, he held, any psychological phenomenon is synonymous with the corresponding set of operations. Both logical positivism and operationism combined with behaviorism in an effort to objectify psychology by stating everything in "cgs" terms.

In the 1950s and early 1960s, operationism became differentiated into two rather distinct phases. One was *philosophical,* or *prescriptive* operationism, a continuation of the earlier trend and of the positivism of the previous century. It involved full espousal of the strong meaning of the term "operational definition," in the sense of a genuine identity between concept and operation, and continues in the philosophy of logical analysis. (Thus for Bridgman, in 1927, there was no real meaning to the idea of the other side of the moon; but nowadays there is one, since it has been defined by being photographed and otherwise explored.) The other branch, of more concern to psychology proper, might be called *methodological,* or *descriptive* operationism. It does not commit itself on the question of identity between concept and operation in a logical sense, but accepts the need for operational definitions—or better perhaps, operational characterizations or operational specifications—of concepts if one is to work with them empirically. Concept and operation may not be identical, but at least the operation must "fit" the concept to some extent. Virtually all psychologists who engage in empirical work accept this kind of operationism whether they know it or not, since you need an operational "handle" for research concepts if you are going to work with them empirically.

A related development is the notion of "converging operations" or of "operational triangulation," that is, using several simultaneous operational characterizations of the "same" concept. As long as one accepts that a concept may have a kind of "surplus meaning" over and beyond its definition by a given operation, it becomes reasonable, as it were, to attack the concept simultaneously from several different directions. None of them is then considered to be exhaustive, to be "the" definition of the concept, but each taps the concept in a slightly different way. Rather sophisticated techniques, most of them using correlations among different measures of presumably the "same" underlying trait, dimension, or concept, were being developed in the middle of the twentieth century by such methodologists as Wendell R. Garner, Donald T. Campbell, and Donald W. Fiske.

## THE SPREAD OF THE EMPIRICAL METHOD

One could argue that progress occurs when an operation is invented for a concept which could not previously be specified. The early experimentalists had devised methods for measuring and manipulating the "basic processes" of sensation, perception, reaction, and memory. Later, what Wundt called the "higher mental processes," as well as other complex phenomena, were subjected to empirical investigation. Consider a few selected examples of empirical progress in some of the more complex areas of psychology.

Empirical inroads into the field of personality were first made by the late nineteenth-century psychologists interested in individual differences—Hall, Cattell, Galton, and others, and at least one of the roads was paved by Alfred Binet's (1857–1911) and Lewis Terman's (1877–1956) thorough development of the concept of an intelligence test. The projective methods, in the hands of Hermann Rorschach (1884–1922), a Swiss Jungian psychiatrist who shortly before his early death developed the ink-blot test to tap the structure of personality, and of Henry A. Murray (1893–　　), an American psychologist who a decade or so later devised the Thematic Apperception Test to get at its contents, grew into vastly popular techniques for the assessment of intricate, subtle aspects of personality. During the 1940s Robert R. Sears (1908–　　) and others tried to restate some psychoanalytic concepts, such as projection, into empirically clear-cut operations, and performed some ingenious experiments which almost succeeded in bringing the psychoanalytic theory into the mainstream of experimental psychology.

The complex field of cognition and thought, particularly as it develops in childhood, was cultivated for more than a half century by Jean Piaget (1896–　　), an inventive European investigator who devised many ingenious experimental situations designed to discover whether a child is capable of using various concepts such as the conservation of mass, of transposition, and the like; he worked out a theory of developmental stages, such that a given concept cannot be used unless the child already understands some ontogenetically and logically prior concept. The psychology of thought had come under empirical study in the work of the Würzburg school and of the gestalt psychologists. Concept formation became a major focus for experimental work after the pioneer efforts of Clark Hull and of Edna Heidbreder; later it merged with the area of verbal learning, an outgrowth of Ebbinghaus's work, and continued to attract large numbers of devoted researchers.

Perhaps historians of the future will be able to write that David McClelland (1917–　　) has done for the study of human motivation what Hermann Ebbinghaus did for human learning and memory. Using Henry Murray's Thematic Apperception Test, McClelland and his students developed crude but reasonably reliable quantitative techniques for measuring such complex human motives as the need for achievement, the need for affiliation, and the need for power, and have manipulated them experimentally. In this way, motivation and personality were brought into the laboratory, rather than remaining in the clinic or in the armchair.

A similar development was brought about in the study of meaning by Charles E. Osgood (1916–    ), a prolific systematic psychologist within the atomistic, behavioristic, experimental tradition. He developed the semantic differential, an ingenious yet simple method for measuring connotative meaning, opening up to quantitative empirical investigation an area that before had remained in the province of the philosopher or the linguist, and helping to launch a new interdisciplinary research area: psycholinguistics.

Social psychology too had become empirical. Sophisticated techniques for the measurement of attitudes were developed by Louis L. Thurstone (1887–1955), Rensis Likert (1903–    ), E. S. Bogardus, and others, and such processes as the influence of group pressure on individual opinion were taken into the laboratory by Solomon Asch (1907–    ), Muzafer Sherif (1906–    ), and Richard Crutchfield (1912–    ), to name only a few. The fields of prejudice, of social perception, of the authoritarian personality, of group interaction, group structure, and group dynamics, partly through the impetus of the followers of Kurt Lewin, each became major research foci.

Physiological psychology also developed along new lines, with some exciting discoveries which the historian of the future may well come to consider major landmarks in psychology's evolution. David Krech (1909–    ) and his collaborators studied the relation between chemical events in the brain and various aspects of behavior, particularly learning and intelligence. The role of DNA and RNA in the neural correlate of learning generated too much excitement. James Olds (1922–    ) discovered that electrical stimulation of certain parts of the deep brain can be reinforcing, leading to a modern experimental and physiological version of the ancient hedonistic question of the nature, causes, and concomitants of pleasure. D. H. Hubel and T. N. Wiesel in the early 1960s found cells in the visual brain that respond not to brightness as such, but to complex stimulus characteristics such as the angle of a line and its direction of motion. All of these findings reflect the renewed interest in the relation between processes in the central nervous system and behavior.

These are, of course, only a few selected examples. Overall, the conquest of ever wider terrain by the empirical method wrought a major change in the twentieth-century image of the behavioral sciences. At the turn of the century, when the term "behavioral sciences" did not even exist, psychology was mostly limited to the study of simple sensory processes, memory, and reaction time, but by the middle of the century such humanly "charged" areas as learning, thinking, cognition, motivation, personality, abnormal behavior, and social phenomena were being taken out of the philosopher's study, the physician's consulting room, and the minister's pulpit to be subjected to the impartial scrutiny of the quantitative, objective scientist. It had become atavistic to characterize some subpart of psychology as "experimental"; experimental psychology no longer existed as a separate field. Empirical methods had invaded just about *all* areas of psychology.

## PROFESSIONALISM

The trend to professionalism resulted in a major, rapid change in the identity of the psychologist. About 1930 almost everyone who considered himself a psychologist was still in an academic position, but by 1950 more than half of all psychologists were working outside university settings. Most of the nonacademics were in some form of clinical work—and the first psychological clinic had been founded as late as 1896 by Lightner Witmer at the University of Pennsylvania.

Clinical psychology was given a nudge during the First World War with the need to develop tests for recruits, and an even larger push during the Second World War, both with the further development of tests and with the need for treatment of psychological casualties. Soon the American Psychological Association saw the need to formalize and regulate the rapidly growing practice of clinical psychology, and set up the American Board of Examiners in Professional Psychology, to examine and award diplomas to qualified practitioners. The Veterans Administration, state hospitals, community clinics, and other institutions created more positions for clinical psychologists than even the extraordinarily rapid rise in the number of trained clinical psychologists could cope with—and at the present writing the demand continues to outstrip the supply.

But the service functions of psychologists were not limited to clinical work. Industrial psychology produced human factors specialists, who helped in the design of devices so that they will fit the characteristics of the human operator or consumer; management consultants, who worked with problems of labor relations, employee personnel, industrial organization, and executive placement; advertising consultants; attitude change experts; as well as still other specialists. Survey research became a major enterprise, with efforts to predict everything from election results to consumer reaction to a new product or the success of a new advertising appeal. Military psychologists engaged in personnel work, in devising training methods, in practical studies of leadership, and in psychological problems created by the space age, such as the study of small group interaction under conditions of long-term confinement in a limited environment, as well as research on human behavior under entirely new ecological circumstances. And there are still other ways in which the psychologist uses his particular training, perspective, and experience in the service of his society—in consultation to government, in applied problems of animal behavior, in consultation to the schools, in the understanding of the special problems of disabled people, and so on.

## QUANTIFICATION

Psychology became increasingly quantitative in its orientation. The use of statistical methods for the evaluation of empirical results by virtually everyone hardly needs mention. Quite aside from the mental testing movement and the ubiquity of statistics, there was a strong and growing tendency to construct theories having the precision of mathematical formulations. Major impetus was given this development by the invention of information theory by communications engineers like Claude E. Shannon and mathematicians like Norbert Wiener (1894–1964), the founder of the new discipline of cybernetics; information theory, or concepts akin to those in the theory, were applied to a wide variety of problems in sensation, perception, and learning by people like George A. Miller (1920–    ) and Fred Attneave (1919–    ). Sensation, already quantitatively approached by investigators a century earlier, became again a major focus of mathematical thought in psychology with the development of sensory scaling by S. S. Stevens, W. R. Garner (1921–    ), J. G. Beebe-Center (1897–1958), and others. There has also been much interest in mathematical learning theory, beginning perhaps with Clark Hull (although the trend can be traced back at least to Herbart), with the construction of mathematical models of learning by Robert Bush (1920–    ) and Frederick Mosteller (1916–    ), and by William Estes (1919–    ), Frank Restle (1927–    ), and many others. Decision theory was applied to human problem solving and troubleshooting by individuals like Ward Edwards (1927–    ). And in social psychology a variety of "balance models" had been proposed by people like Helen Peak (1900–    ), Fritz Heider (1896–    ), and Theodore Newcomb (1903–    ). One version of balance theory holds, for example, that if A and B like each other, and A and C dislike each other, the structure of the trio A, B, and C will be relatively stable if B and C dislike each other, but unstable if they do not.

The availability of the modern high-speed computer produced an entire new research field: the computer simulation of higher mental processes in humans. Thus there were, for example, problem-solving programs, chess-playing programs, and programs to generate new logical proofs, written by such leading figures in the field as Herbert A. Simon (1916–    ). The hope appeared to be that a theory as concrete and detailed as one required as a basis for preparing such programs, whose outputs are indistinguishable from the behavioral output of the living, thinking, learning human subject, could lead to a better understanding of such complex psychological events in man. Computers also contributed to the feasibility of factor analytic methodology, since a factor analysis, which used to take days or weeks on a desk calculator, could be performed by an accomplished computer in a matter of minutes.

## EXISTENTIALISM

Later psychology, then, had become operational, empirical, service-oriented and quantitative. It was sophisticated. But there was also another trend, which did not fit into this picture, and which may, indeed, be seen as a reaction to it: existentialism. The existentialist movement in the United States had its roots in the theology of Sören Kierkegaard and later of Martin Buber, and in the philosophy of Jean-Paul Sartre.

Rollo May (1909–    ), Abraham Maslow (1916–    ), Carl Rogers (1902–    ), and other American psychologists were deeply concerned with the attempt to discover the identity of the individual, the meaning of life and existence, with a view of man as in a quandary which requires him constantly to make choices and decisions, usually in the absence of sufficient relevant information. A reaffirmation of man's fundamental humanity, an existentialist position holds that man is basically free, but that recognition of this freedom, of the knowledge that one is and does what one chooses to be and do, can be a source of deep anxiety.

Thus existentialism was on the fringe of psychology proper, much as psychoanalysis was. It was, in psychology, mostly a protest movement against critical empiricism and scientific materialism. Yet it captured the interest of many psychologists, especially those concerned with clinical or philosophical problems.

## AN EVALUATION

Psychology is a fast-moving, fast-changing discipline. The prevalent theory of the day before yesterday became a historical curiosity yesterday; the ingenious new gadget of yesterday is a crude horse-and-buggy device today; and the exciting research field to which everybody flocks today will look like a somewhat misguided and outmoded fad tomorrow. Theories, instruments, research fads, and various subtle but far-reaching connotative aspects of the general psychological climate change at a pace that may seem alarming to the psychologist. For what he himself learned thirty or ten or even two years ago tends to be hopelessly out of date today.

There is a great deal of rapid change, yes. The methods, the orientation, the detailed problems, are constantly shifting. Yet in a sense the basic problem remains the same. Man has always been interested in himself. For thousands of years he has speculated about the nature of human nature. But it is only in the last century or so that the effects of a fundamental methodological revolution in the study of man have been clearly felt.

Man is, of course, still interested in man, but he is no longer content to do nothing but spin long-winded subtle speculations. The behavioral sciences have left the armchair and entered the laboratory; reliance on the wise experienced mind, equipped with oratory and quill pen and paper, has given way to reliance on the impersonal scientist with his precise measurements, his cold numbers, and his electronic computers.

Before the turn of the century, man's ineffable rich nature was safe from the probings of the aseptic scientist; everybody knew that science could never penetrate the peculiarly human characteristics of man and degrade him to become nothing more than just another inert part of the world of the microscope and the sliderule. The dignity of man, the only possessor in the universe of the Cartesian unextended substance—soul—was unassailable.

The rallying cry of the revolution in twentieth-century behavioral science is that nothing is holy. There is nothing about man to which the cold, dispassionate empirical approach cannot be applied. Measurement, experiment, and formal prediction have infiltrated virtually all areas. Man as a sensing, learning, motivated social being was wrested from the cloud-bound arms of the philosopher and theologian and dissected under cold controlled conditions by that twentieth-century Darwinian mutation, the behavioral scientist. Disquieting though it was to those who wished to preserve an anthropocentric view of the universe, the conclusion gradually became inescapable: there is nothing about man's deepest feelings, thoughts, values, and behavior which cannot be subjected to the scientist's no-nonsense scrutiny.

The revolution has not occurred without strong opposition. It is safer and perhaps more pleasant to speculate comfortably from the podium, the armchair, or the pulpit than to risk one's convictions by examining them objectively, empirically. Argument can always be met with argument, but objective empirical data are relatively immune to wanton bias.

The revolution in behavioral science, like many revolutions, did not occur overnight. Rumblings can be found in the eighteenth and nineteenth centuries, and even earlier. The beginnings were modest, but the infiltration of the scientific method into new areas snowballed geometrically. The amount of new territory covered in the twentieth century was truly awesome.

The distinctiveness of man in contrast with all other animals had already received a shattering blow in the Darwinian revolution, which pointed to a structural continuity between man and other animals. It was not long before the Darwinian approach was applied to behavioral as well as to morphological characteristics. Comparative psychology began late in the nineteenth century and became a major endeavor during the twentieth. Comparisons between man and other animals became a matter of measurement rather than conjecture, and man did not always come off better in these comparisons.

In 1900, although the seeds of the revolution had already taken root, things still seemed fairly safe for a mystical humanist. To be sure, mental chronometry was well established, some rather elementary sensory and associational processes had been brought into the laboratory, and a few crude experiments had been performed on the problem-solving abilities of animals. It seemed a far—and a safe—cry from these isolated bits of superficial information to a full-scale invasion of the private domain of man's essential humanity. But quietly, perhaps insidiously, this invasion occurred during the twentieth century, and victory appeared close to complete.

The modern behavioral scientist can claim that there is nothing human that is alien to him: he can study empirically virtually any aspect of man he wishes to. The twentieth century has seen studies of social phenomena, personality, cognitive processes, and complex personality deviations. Psychologists look into psycholinguists, psychotherapy, lobotomy, tranquilizing drugs, dreams. All are now studied, not in a literary or philosophical vein, but scientifically.

Some diehard humanists may come up with the vague but strong feeling that all of this somehow does not really get at the essence of man. It may be quite interesting, but somehow tangential, irrelevant to an understanding of the nature of human nature. The behavioral scientist replies by saying that he would like to know what it is about man that this approach misses. Specify what is lacking, and we can work on ways to get at it. As soon as it is specified, it becomes accessible to scientific investigation.

Perhaps the revolution in twentieth-century behavioral science can, like the Renaissance, be characterized as an adoption of the research attitude rather than an attitude of venerating argument or authority. The research attitude means raising two questions with regard to any assertion. First, Is it true? Second, and far more important, How can one find out if it is true? What kinds of measurements will get at the heart of the assertion, and test it validly? What kinds of operations can be used to check the statement? Faith, precedent, authority, argument, and fad are out; they are much too subject to predilection, bias, and wishful thinking. Only an objective empirical investigation can give trustworthy results that will stay reasonably put. As indicated earlier, nothing is immune to the research attitude's questions: Is it true? How can I find out if it is true? Nothing is holy when it comes to the application of the scientific method.

The revolution in twentieth-century behavioral science, then, seems very nearly complete. The day of the armchair is past. Everything about human behavior, including how social, philosophical, and religious values develop, can be subjected to the scientist's cold scrutiny. Maybe the role of philosophy, of humanism, and of religion is to raise important questions, but science is the method of choice for answering them.

Paradoxical as it may seem at first glance, a dispassionate scientific approach is, in the last analysis, also the most humanitarian one. We will be in the best position to help people if we know what works, what effects something has when we are trying to help troubled souls get along in this world. The revolutionary maintains that science is apt to be more helpful in this vital endeavor than are magic, wishful thinking, philosophy, or theology.

So here is one man's impression of the state of psychology today. Psychology is a sophisticated, quantitative, empirical science, one that is growing rapidly, and one that can be applied, at least tentatively, to help in the solution of many of society's practical problems. It is not a body of established truths, of clinical wisdom, of philosophical speculations, but a complex, vigorous, powerful set of sophisticated methods for the discovery of fundamental relationships that can be of great significance for every man, and a set of useful scientific generalizations—but each generalization has a probabilistic tag on it: none is absolute. Psychology is an approach, a way of tackling problems and thinking about them. Psychology is making tremendous strides; anyone involved in the field can take pride in the power, humility, breadth, and success of the psychology of today.

## SUMMARY OF PART III

The middle of the first half of the twentieth century was the age of schools. Wundtian structuralism flourished in the rigid systematization of Titchener. Functionalism, which was more concerned with the use of mind than with its content, developed both at Chicago under Dewey, Angell, Carr, and Mead, and at Columbia under Cattell, Thorndike, and Woodworth. Behaviorism, which rejected the study of consciousness and concentrated instead solely upon the study of objective, behavioral phenomena, grew out of functionalism, was popularized by John B. Watson, and matured with Lashley, Hunter, Guthrie, Hull, Tolman, and Skinner. The gestalt school objected to the elementarism of structuralism, functionalism, and behaviorism, and emphasized the relational determination of psychological events; the leaders of this movement were Wertheimer, Koffka, Köhler, and Lewin. Growing out of a different tradition, psychoanalysis attempted a full understanding of the human mind in all of its complexity, with intricate theories developed by Freud, Jung, and Adler; the Neo-Freudians emphasized the social determinants of deep personality phenomena.

The age of schools did not last beyond about 1940. By this time psychology had become an objective science, and people were concentrating on their own particular research areas. A new, practical operational methodology branched off from operational philosophy. Piaget studied children; Rorschach's test was used extensively; new inroads were made on neurological correlates of behavior by Krech, Olds, and others; McClelland measured motivation, and Osgood meaning. Psychology found itself being used by society in a wide variety of areas, and became increasingly quantitative. If any pervasive philosophy was characteristic of the efforts of psychologists in the latter part of the twentieth century, it was that there is nothing about human behavior and experience which cannot be studied scientifically.

# References

Boring, E. G. *A history of experimental psychology.* (2nd ed.) New York: Appleton-Century-Crofts, 1950 (a).

Boring, E. G. Great men and scientific progress. *Proceedings of the American Philosophical Society,* 1950 (b). Vol. 94, pp. 339–351.

Boring, E. G., & Lindzey, G. *A history of psychology in autobiography.* Vol. 5. New York: Appleton-Century-Crofts, 1967.

Chaplin, J. P., and Krawiec, T. S. *Systems and theories of psychology.* (2nd ed.) New York: Holt, Rinehart and Winston, 1968.

Dennis, W. (Ed.) *Readings in the history of psychology.* New York: Appleton-Century-Crofts, 1948.

Hall, C. S. & Lindzey, G. *Theories of personality.* New York: Wiley, 1957.

Heidbreder, Edna. *Seven psychologies.* New York: Appleton-Century-Crofts, 1933.

Herrnstein, R. J., & Boring, E. G. (Eds.) *A source book in the history of psychology.* Cambridge, Mass.: Harvard University Press, 1965.

Hilgard, E. R., & Bower, G. *Theories of learning.* (3rd ed.) New York: Appleton-Century-Crofts, 1966.

Koch, S. (Ed.) *Psychology: A study of a science.* New York: McGraw-Hill, 1959–1964. 6 vols.

Marx, M. H., & Hillix, W. A. *Systems and theories in psychology.* New York: McGraw-Hill, 1963.

Miller, G. A. *Psychology: The science of mental life.* New York: Harper & Row, 1962.

Murchison, C. A. (Ed.) *History of psychology in autobiography.* Worcester, Mass.: Clark University Press, 1932–1952. 4 vols.

Murphy, G. *Historical introduction to modern psychology.* (Rev. ed.) New York: Harcourt, Brace & World, 1949.

Postman, L. (Ed.) *Psychology in the making: Histories of selected research problems.* New York: Knopf, 1962.

Sargent, S. S., & Stafford, K. R. *Basic teachings of the great psychologists.* (Rev. ed.) Garden City, N. Y.: Doubleday, 1965.

Shipley, T. (Ed.) *Classics in psychology.* New York: Philosophical Library, 1961.

Watson, R. I. *The great psychologists: From Aristotle to Freud.* (2nd ed.) Philadelphia: Lippincott, 1968.

Wolman, B. B. *Contemporary theories and systems in psychology.* New York: Harper & Row, 1960.

Woodworth, R. S., & Sheehan, Mary R. *Contemporary schools of psychology.* (3rd ed.) New York: Ronald Press, 1964.

# Index

# Index

any study on the tendency of psychology writers to oversimplify?